Madeline,

May God bless you
as you make every day
significant.

Esther Hughes

One Day:

The Difference a Day Can Make

Esther Hughes

PublishAme
Baltimor

First printing

ISBN: 1-4137-4038-3
PUBLISHED BY
PUBLISHAMERICA, LLLP.
www.publishamerica.com
Baltimore

Printed in the United States of America

I dedicate this book to the people
who made these dates significant days in my life:

October 21, 1965	*– My parents for bringing me into the world*
March 1971	*– Christ for coming into my life*
June 24, 1983	*– TCCS Class of 1983*
May 19, 1990	*– Dan for his lifelong love*
October 26, 1995	*– Tyler for being our firstborn*
June 8, 1997	*– Alexia for being our daughter*
May 18, 2000	*– Justin for being our baby*
January 8, 2002	*– Dr. Beth DuPree, Dr. Rob Skalicky and Dr. Angela DeMichele for giving me hope*

Acknowledgements

Many individuals have been a part of this book, and here is my chance to thank them.

Thanks first goes to my family members who have been there for me. To my parents, Ruth and Wendell Garrison, for loving and supporting me throughout my life. Thank you to each of my siblings and their spouses; Eileen and Ken Codner; Miriam and Doug Pipher; Paul and Terri Garrison; and Joel and Debbie Garrison, you guys are awesome and I love you. Thank you to my parents-in-law, Betty and Jack Hughes, for supporting me through this process. Thank you to my "sisters," Kelly Hughes and Colleen and Jason Hessenthaler—you guys are terrific.

Thanks also to my writing buddies, Marti Shadle, Sheree Woodington and Arianne Hegeman—the three of you were huge encouragers and Part III was a result of our brainstorming session in the library snack room. Lisa Marie Beamer and Mary Ann Diorio for coaching and mentoring me from the rough stages of my writing. Sharon Norris Elliott for teaching the Beginner's Track at Sandy Cove in 1998.

To the staff at PublishAmerica for giving me a chance and believing in this work. Jeni Watterson, thank you for that initial email!

Most importantly, my husband, Dan, who did more than encourage me. He read, edited, inspired, contributed and loved me through this book and helped immensely with our three greatest blessings—Tyler, Lexi and Justin!

Thanks to God for the gift of life.

ONE DAY: THE DIFFERENCE A DAY CAN MAKE
TABLE OF CONTENTS

Introduction

Great opportunities come to all, but many do not know they have met them. The only preparation to take advantage of them is simple fidelity to watch what each day brings.
— Albert E. Dunning

WHAT DID YOU DO TODAY? That's a common question asked each day. We want to know what difference *today* makes in a life. Today can make all the difference in our lives, yet daily living takes over and makes us forget the importance of one single day in one life...each life. For the majority of us, we live in a phase of "cruise control." We do not think of the meaning of every moment and how each day is significant, and how a matter of 24 hours can play an important role in our lifelong search for the next pursuit.

To make my point, watch the evening news and note the difference TODAY made in the lives of many. The news is filled with information pertaining to other people and what happened to them today. There are automobile accidents where individuals are harmed or, worse yet, killed. There are house fires where people are burnt or displaced from their homes. There are murders, rapes, wars, airplane crashes, robberies and the list of bad news goes on. Also in the news are announcements of prominent births, marriages, divorces, and accomplishments. The next time you watch the news, think about the difference a few hours made in the lives of those who are the news. But beware, this is depressing, unless you are prepared for TODAY.

Throughout the pages of this book we will reflect on the days of Americans' lives to provoke thought in how you choose to live your life and what dates are important in your journey. The important days could be your birth; graduation from high school or college; the day you moved away from home; your wedding day; the days your children were born; the day you are informed of a life-threatening disease; the day you lost a parent, spouse, child, sibling, or best friend. We all have specific days in our lives that were more important than others, so we know the difference that one day can make in our lives.

Each of us has a story inside us to tell, and while some may be more interesting than others, there is a story there nonetheless. Every day that we live is important because it creates the story of our lives and the lives of those we bring into the world in following generations. For many, crucial circumstances thrust them into the public spotlight that gives their story an extra punch, yet for others, no outlandish circumstance ever occurs. Nevertheless, the significance of your life is important.

The dates chosen for this book are only a handful of significant dates in history. They were chosen to highlight how the importance of certain decisions made can transform history in a matter of moments. Although there are thousands of other noteworthy dates and events not included in this work, the purpose of this book is not to outline the key dates in America's history but to show how one day can change the course of a country, the path of an individual's life, and the destiny of all.

Part I
Significant Dates in the History of the United States

Courage is not simply one of the virtues,
but the form of every virtue at the testing point.
— C. S. Lewis

THE BIRTH OF THIS NATION began over one hundred years before sovereignty was gained. During that period of time there were many prominent dates that marked the transformation of an uncivilized land and brought about the super power country that the United States is today. It did not happen on one day, but it was a culmination of days that brought about the world as we know it today. From the discovery by Christopher Columbus to the sailing of the *Mayflower* to today, this country has been formed by dates that have played an integral role in the development and molding of American culture. The determination set forth by the original pilgrims is not lost on the events that take place today. It was with much bloodshed, loss of life, hunger, and hard work that gave us the wonderful country that is the home of the brave and the free. Travel with me over the next few chapters and discover the importance that one day played in our American heritage.

Chapter 1
July 4, 1776–The Birth of a Nation

We are not weak if we make a proper use of those means
which the God of Nature has placed in our power... The
battle, sir, is not to the strong alone; it is to the vigilant,
the active, the brave.

–Patrick Henry

WHEN THE PILGRIMS ARRIVED ON this continent in 1620, they were searching for a better life away from the rule of the King of England. Their purpose was to find a land where they could worship and live freely. Through countless difficulties and much loss of life, they were able to accomplish their goal; however, it took over 150 years for the nation to be established and to break away from England's rule.

There were numerous twists and turns that led to the beginning of our country, but the date that we have come to recognize and celebrate our independence as a sovereign nation takes place each year on July 4th. When we celebrate the Fourth, we often think of patriotic parades, barbecues, baseball games, vacations and fireworks. Just knowing that we are celebrating the birth of our nation and its independence is enough to declare an annual tradition, but we should never forget the magnitude and cost with which our freedom was gained and is still maintained today.

The American Revolution began in April of 1775 after years of dissatisfaction by the Colonial Americans with the King of

England. Every year we honor that day in 1776 when great leaders such as John Adams, Benjamin Franklin, John Hancock, Robert Livingston, Roger Sherman, Thomas Jefferson and several others came together as a unified body and signed *The Declaration of Independence*. Even though the Revolutionary War raged on for five more years after *The Declaration* was signed, that *one* day has perpetually affected our country. The decisions made by the Continental Congress and the men who signed the wonderfully crafted document by Thomas Jefferson changed the course of the world forever.

Did those men have an inkling as to the impact that one day would make in the course of history? Did they realize the United States of America would become the most powerful nation in years to come? They may have dreamed of the outcome of that one day, but did they know what the date July 4th would mean each year for coming generations? Despite their ability to clearly visualize or predict the future, they stood firm on their belief that this group of people who had settled in the 13 American Colonies desired the right to live their lives without the control of the British Empire. Or as Thomas Jefferson more eloquently stated: "When in the Course of human events, it becomes necessary for one people to dissolve the political bands which have connected them with another..."[1] Our independence as a nation began. The impact of that *one* day and the bravery of the signers of *The Declaration of Independence* is one of the single most historical events since the beginning of time.

Some of the signers were not present to sign *The Declaration of Independence* on July 4, 1776, but signed it in early August. However, July 4 was the date that was adopted

---

[1] Jerome Agel and Mort Gerberg, *The U.S. Declaration of Independence for Everyone,* (New York: The Berkley Publishing Group, 2001), 41.

for the signatures and for the Congress to force the King of England into realizing their intent. There were scores of momentous events that led up to July 4, 1776, but the document that was signed that day informed the King and all of Great Britain that the members of the Continental Congress were willing to lay down their lives for the sovereignty of the colonies and the birth of their new nation. Those men who signed *The Declaration* knew that if the British caught them, they could endure hardship and even death for treason. In fact, five of them were eventually caught and tortured.

John Hancock

The first signature placed on *The Declaration* was that of John Hancock, who represented Massachusetts, and who allegedly made a statement suggesting that King George would be able to read his signature because of its boldness. The prominent nature of his signature clearly indicated that he was a leader who was not going to be thwarted or threatened by the King or the powers to be from Great Britain. Most of us are acquainted with who John Hancock was because of the use of his name as a synonym for the word "signature," but he is also known for the vast role he played in the business of Boston and the politics of Massachusetts.

Hancock's original intentions were to remain loyal to Britain because he relished the elements of high society and would have liked to be a loyal British subject. However, when England started placing high taxes on the colonial merchants and planters, he eventually joined the rebel crusade in order to avoid losing more of his wealth. Due to the uncompromising British Parliament, John Hancock not only joined the Revolutionary cause, but he gradually gained control of the rebellion and, in the end, gave the people of Massachusetts a stable and independent government.

Once he realized there was to be no compromise by Britain,

the independence did not come soon enough for him. Looking at his biographical data, we can rest assured that this first and largest signatory definitely knew what he was doing when he signed the document. He undoubtedly had a mission of gaining independence and he intended to make sure that happened. Not only did he know the consequences of signing *The Declaration of Independence*, but he was aware of the impact the document would have for generations to come.

John Hancock was no saint in his business dealings, and was known to be a hardheaded and manipulative businessman, so some accounts about his life believe his allegiance to the Revolutionary cause had more to do with money and power than liberty. Maybe that was the case for other Founding Fathers as well; however, the fact remains that because of that one day and that one document, we do celebrate independence and liberty in what Americans believe to be the greatest nation on earth.[2]

Robert Morris

Another signer, Robert Morris, from Pennsylvania was noted as being a wealthy businessman in Philadelphia before his political career started in 1775. His signature is to the right of John Hancock's and easy to read. Morris was an importer who was hit very hard by the *Stamp Act,* which thrust him into siding with the colonials. As a member of the Continental Congress he was personally involved in raising the funds and finding provisions for the Continental Army. Not only did he raise money, but he loaned his own money to the Revolutionary cause. He also devised the plan that, once approved by Congress, became the establishment of The Bank

---

[2] Harlow Giles Unger, *John Hancock: Merchant King and American Patriot*, (New York: John Wiley & Sons, 2000).

of North America. This institution handled the continuing financial needs of the Revolutionary War and aided in bringing stability to the colonial economy. Eventually, the bank was what established the credit of the United States with the European nations.

Robert Morris personally funded so much of the war effort that he never regained his wealth after the war ended. He died in poverty in 1806. As a founding father, Morris definitely realized the impact of *The Declaration of Independence*, but may not have been able to comprehend what that one day would represent to the nation and to the world over 200 years later.[3]

Charles Carroll

Franklin, Jefferson, Adams and Hancock are often the first names we associate with the signers of *The Declaration of Independence*; however, they were only a few of the signers whose mark became famous. There were 56 signatures in all and each of the men made an important point by signing the document. Charles Carroll from Maryland is the fourth signature below John Hancock's in the center of the document.

Carroll was born in Annapolis, Maryland, to a wealthy family. His formal education began at eight years old when he was shipped to France where he attended Jesuits' College at St. Omar, France. His studies abroad continued through his teen and young adult years, and the young refined gentlemen returned to his home in his late twenties during the politically heated days of the *Stamp Act*. It is believed that Charles Carroll immediately became involved in the Revolutionary cause and

---

[3]Jerome Agel and Mort Gerberg, *The U.S. Declaration of Independence for Everyone,* (New York: The Berkley Publishing Group, 2001), 60.

built relationships with other patriots. He advocated the war and the separation of Great Britain before Maryland decided to send a delegate to the First Continental Congress. Carroll, however, remained committed to the Revolution and participated in many acts to further the cause of freedom. Although he was not at the meeting when *The Declaration* was voted on, he was there on July 4, 1776, to sign the document.

Carroll was the only Roman Catholic signer, and he was also the last surviving signatory when he died at the age of 95 in 1832.[4]

Thomas Jefferson

Thomas Jefferson was a member of the Continental Congress representing his home state of Virginia when he was selected to draft America's birth certificate. He was known as an eloquent writer, thus he was the perfect choice. His initial draft of the document had scratched out words and phrases just like a rough draft for any document would have. As he wrote this document, he was well aware of the reason such a document was needed because he had been dedicated to the Patriot's cause and wanted freedom from England's firm hand of power upon early America.

While he crafted the document, Thomas Jefferson may have known the initial goal that *The Declaration* would have for the current generation and even his children's generation, but to become one of the most powerful sovereign nations on earth may have only been a dream. However, the well-phrased article spoke volumes for the Patriots of that time and is still relevant for today with its phraseology exclaiming, "We hold these truths to be self-evident, that all men are created equal, that they are endowed by their Creator with certain unalienable

---

[4] Ibid., 53.

Rights, that among these are Life, Liberty and the pursuit of Happiness."[5]

That famous phrase has been carried forth from generation to generation and was the beginning of the American Dream as we now know it in the twenty-first century. It all started with a few men's vision for a future bright with promise and *one day* when Congress stood together in adopting the important document and its words as a beginning to freedom and sovereignty.

There were numerous noteworthy events that led up to July 4th and their relevance is what brought about what we now recognize as Independence Day. The significance of that date is because of choices made on the days, weeks, months and years that led up to July 4, 1776. It is one momentous day to each American life because it was the beginning of our freedom. It marked the establishment of the life that we treasure today. One *day* does make a big difference and forces us to recognize the need to live freely and reverently, which is of great importance today in a society that is far richer, better educated and more technologically advanced.

It all started on an insignificant day that became significant by an ongoing cause for freedom and independence. Today, over 225 years later, *The Declaration* still stands strong, unfaltering to the attacks by other countries who would love to destroy what we hold dear. Their evil intents are pushed aside because Americans still stand up for *The Declaration of Independence* made on July 4, 1776.

---

[5]Ibid., 41.

Chapter 2
July 3, 1863—The Battle of Gettysburg

It is well that war is so terrible, or we should grow too fond of it.
—Robert E. Lee

THE CIVIL WAR WAS A drastic measure that brought change to the hearts and minds of the people of our country. It is hard to imagine what it was like living during those trying and traumatic days when our country was divided. Numerous lives were changed by mere feet, yards and miles because families were fighting for their cause against one another. The trauma that our young country experienced during the Civil War deprived America from celebrating freedom and independence. It took far too many years after the war had ended to repair the brokenness of the special unity which had brought the nation together. The war lasted four long years, yet several historians believe that the turning point of the Civil War took place in a small farming town in Pennsylvania that lasted three days. The Battle of Gettysburg's significance changed the face of the war and our nation. For the thousands of soldiers that died during those three days, the significance of their cause was unfortunately necessary to overcome the division of the Union.

July 1, 1863, marked the first day of the Battle of Gettysburg. The residents of the small town had first encountered the Confederates just a few days before the battle actually started, but July 1, 1863, marked its inception when the two sides collided. The tragic events that took place on the battlefields were gruesome enough, yet there were tragedies off the battlefield that left women, children and civilians scarred for life. The battle left behind a town in ruin and mourning and a broken country. This town still holds a deep history marked by the blood of Americans who believed in their own cause—two causes of dividing intent.

Mary Virginia Wade "Jennie"

On the morning of July 3, 1863, Jennie Wade awoke to a third day of baking bread for tired and hungry Union soldiers. For the first two days of battle, Jennie, her mother and two younger brothers had spent their time in the home of Jennie's sister, Georgia, helping her after the birth of her baby. While aiding her sister, Jennie helped the Union soldiers by offering them fresh baked bread and cold water. What would be significant about this day was unforeseen to Jennie as she read her Bible before that morning's baking began. At 8:30 a.m. Jennie's life was suddenly taken when a sharpshooter's bullet tore through two wooden doors before stopping below Jennie's shoulder blade and pierced her heart. The 20-year-old woman—engaged to Jack Skelly, who was a member of the 2nd Pennsylvania Infantry—had faithfully served her sister and the Union soldiers, yet during the last day of battle, her destiny was suddenly changed.

That day the only civilian killed during the Battle of Gettysburg was a young woman serving others and unassuming of the danger that war brought to her life.[6]

---

[6] Jack McLaughlin, *Gettysburg: The Long Encampment*, (New York: Bonanza Books, 1963) 127.

John Wesley Culp "Wesley"

Wesley Culp was born and raised in Gettysburg where generations of his family had lived. He moved to (West) Virginia in his teen years when the owner of the company he worked for moved his business to Shepherdstown, Virginia. During his childhood, Wesley was friendly with Jennie Wade and Jack Skelly. By the time the Civil War started, Wesley was a resident of West Virginia, so he decided to become a Confederate soldier even though family members and his good friend from Gettysburg were for the Union. On July 3, Wesley battled on Culp's Hill as a member of the 2nd Virginia of the Stonewall Brigade. Wesley was killed on the land that bore his name and where he played and hunted as a child.[7]

Major General George Gordon Meade

This newly selected general had slept little since his appointment to major general on June 27 and, as a new day dawned on July 3rd in Gettysburg, Meade labored over the uncertainty of the day. The West Point graduate faced a most difficult burden when his forces collided with the Confederates at Gettysburg. The fighting had barely ceased on the evening of July 2 when Meade called his corps commanders to his headquarters to gain the status of each of their commands and consult with them about their next move. He knew that the federal casualties had been high and found that more than 18,000 men had been killed, wounded or captured during the two days of fighting. Meade's biggest decision was whether or not he should remain in Gettysburg and whether or not they should remain on the defensive or take an offensive role. The

---

[7] Jeffrey D. Wert, *Gettysburg: Day Three* (New York: Simon & Schuster, 2001), 90.

officers agreed unanimously to defend Gettysburg for at least one more day. As the meeting dispersed, Meade approached Junior Officer John Gibbon, whose Second Corps division defended the center of the Union line where the "small clump of trees" marked the ridge to the west of the army headquarters.

Meade told Gibbon, "If Lee attacks tomorrow, it will be in your front."[8]

Gibbon questioned the general as to why he thought that would be the case and General Meade said, "Because he had made attacks on both our flanks and failed and if he concludes to try it again, it will be on our centre."[9]

Gibbon's response was hopeful that Lee would do just that because he said, "We would defeat him."[10]

Throughout the wee hours of the morning on July 3, 1863, Meade decided that he would initiate the attack on the Confederates. His decision was made because he learned that the Confederates had seized part of the Federal's works on Culp's Hill. However, the Union soldiers waited on Cemetery Ridge and found themselves on the defensive against Lee, Longstreet and Pickett.

Major General George Edward Pickett

The third and final day of battle started with blistering heat and bright sun shining down on the battlefield. General Robert E. Lee commanded General Pickett to take his army of approximately 18,000 men and march a mile through the center of where the Union forces were on Cemetery Ridge to what Lee referred to as "the clump of trees." Lee figured that if Pickett could gain control of this section of the battle zone that

---

[8] Ibid., 17.
[9] Ibid., 17.
[10] Ibid., 17.

the Confederates would reign victorious over the battle and hopefully march all the way to Washington to claim victory. The decisions by General Robert E. Lee, Lieutenant General James Longstreet and Major General Pickett left the Confederate Army defeated.

Accounts of Pickett's skeptic reaction vary. However, he carried out the mission set forth by General Lee and assembled his brigade of 6,300 men along with approximately 12,000 men from other brigades toward Cemetery Ridge stretching almost a mile in the distance. The Confederate advance became known as "Pickett's Charge," even though Pickett himself was not visible to his soldiers during most of the charge. The outcome of the advance may have been different if the promised reinforcements by other brigades had taken place in a timely fashion, but because of the heavy pounding the Union kept delivering, Pickett's men were being hammered to the point of disengagement. The men retreated disheveled, wounded and unorganized. Pickett's division suffered more than 2,700 casualties and knocked out close to 90 percent of his forces in some of the regiments.

Pickett was anguished over the loss of his men and the lack of reinforcements to protect them. After the battle, General Lee encountered General Pickett wandering alone.

"Lee gently admonished him to regroup his division farther to the rear. Looking up abruptly, as though startled by the absurdity of the order, Pickett replied in a low, halting voice that he no longer had a division."[11]

Torn and broken, General Lee had no alternative but to retreat after three days of battle. The road to Washington did not take place. The decision to get to the clump of trees made by Robert E. Lee could have changed the outcome of the Civil

---

[11] Edward G. Lonacre, *Pickett: Leader of the Charge*, (Shippensburg, PA: White Mane Publishing Company, Inc., 1995), 127.

War. It was the decision that many historians believe determined the end to the war even though the war raged on for several more months.

The consequence of one decision on this day in history determined the fate for the United States of America. No doubt the hand of Providence was upon the country during their struggle for the cause, which may be the very reason that it is still called the United States and not broken into two countries. Although General Lee had the advantage at the beginning of the Battle of Gettysburg, clearly some of his decisions and the decisions made by General Meade for the Union soldiers made the difference. One day made all the difference to one nation.

Today we view historical accounts of the Civil War and its various battles that divided our hurting country, but history cannot do justice to the devastated hearts of the men, women and children that endured the most horrific sights that war brings. The division over slavery and maintaining the Union caused so much bloodshed on American soil; still over 150 years later we benefit from how this war shaped our country. We know the outcome of the decisions made by the generals and their impact into what our country is today, but during that time, even those caught in war's crossfires and politics were broken and torn about the future of the United States. Each side had a cause that they believed in. Today we are thankful that the Union was maintained; slavery was banished; and that our country is one sovereign and united nation.

The Civil War occurred over four long years and each battle signified strategic decisions made by both parties; however, a closer look at July 3, 1863, brings the sadness and devastation of a war among Americans home to our hearts. Both sides believed they had a cause worth fighting for, and both sides believed God was with them. God must have been heartbroken to watch his created beings destroy each other with such a vengeance.

———

It was certain decisions made at pivotal moments that determined the outcome of this war and every other war. The loss of human life—no matter what the circumstances is devastating, but war always brings with it a feeling of helplessness, especially a war that was fought to divide a great nation that had claimed sovereignty less than a century before.

Chapter 3
December 7, 1941–A Day of Infamy

We do not live an equal life, but one of contrasts and patchwork; now a little joy, then a sorrow, now a song, then a generous or brave action.
–Ralph Waldo Emerson

THE LUSH TROPICAL LANDSCAPE OF Pearl Harbor, Hawaii, will never be the same. Movies have portrayed the carnage heaped upon the unsuspecting Pacific Naval Fleet, and conflicting reports and conspiracy theories still denigrate into the public about 'what really happened.' Regardless of the theories and what you believe, we know 'what really happened.' Over two thousand American lives were lost suddenly to the relentless blows that the Japanese viciously hailed upon our young service men. Our country's innocence and lackadaisical attitude toward World War II changed in a few short horrific hours of mourning.

The grief-stricken nation suddenly came to life that day and vowed to defeat the Japanese empire that cost them their innocence and lack of zeal for the war effort. Americans proudly hailed their patriotism and young men signed up in droves to serve their country.

Stories swirled from many who witnessed the moments of devastation of the Naval Fleet and to Hickam Field where the Air Force was severely crippled by the continuous blow by the Japanese. The pandemonium of the short time frame rang forth from the shores of Pearl Harbor to the farm towns and cities of the mainland. Each person that was lost that day left behind a grieving family and nation. To this day, December 7, 1941, represents overwhelming sorrow even though World War II was won and evil was overruled. Sometimes, time does not heal all wounds.

Franklin D. Roosevelt

Before December 7, America had been promised by President Franklin D. Roosevelt, "I have said this before, but I shall say it again and again and again. Your boys are not going to be sent into any foreign wars."[12]

The war brought to our land, obviously changed President Roosevelt's heart and mind and the resolve of the American people. In President Roosevelt's famous speech to the Congress on December 8, 1941, he boldly proclaimed, "Yesterday, December 7, 1941, a date which will live in infamy, the United States of America was suddenly and deliberately attacked...."[13]

President Roosevelt was at the White House eating his Sunday dinner from a tray on his desk in his office. He had determined that he was going to rest that day after encountering a tiring week dealing with the war crisis and battling a sinus problem. He had posted a 'do not disturb' order with the switchboard as he hoped to lounge that afternoon; however, as he savored his dinner, the phone harshly rang into the afternoon quietness. The phone call was from Secretary of the Navy, Frank Knox, informing the President of the attack. It was 1:47 p.m. on a sunny December afternoon in Washington, D.C.

---

[12] Andrew Carroll, *War Letters*, (New York: Simon & Schuster, 2001) 184.
[13] Ibid., p. 187.

The President reacted immediately and put his Secretary of the Navy and Secretary of Defense into action to secure other vulnerable areas around the world. The Day of Infamy left a scarred nation and a President reeling with grief.

Admiral William R. Furlong

The admiral walked across the deck of the *Oglala* on what he recalled to be a gorgeous morning. He was awaiting a call for breakfast and noticed that across Battleship Row the quartermaster of each ship was carrying the flag and the buglers were standing by ready to play "To the Colors." The admiral's glance veered to the right when he noticed an incoming plane flying over Ford Island. As the plane dropped a bomb, the admiral thought to himself, "What a stupid, careless pilot, not to have the releasing gear for his bomb properly secured!"[14] The pilot of the plane came so close that Furlong recalled, "I could have hit him with a spud."[15] It only took a moment before Admiral Furlong saw that the plane carried the Japanese 'Rising Sun' insignia and he realized they were under attack.

Before he could order his men to their battle stations, the admiral proudly recalled, "because the men also had heard this explosion and they were busy manning their stations and closing all the doors and manning all the stations immediately and manning the guns."[16]

The U.S. Naval Academy graduate and World War I veteran survived the horrific attack on Pearl Harbor and lived to be 95 years old. He died a decorated war hero in 1976, and is

---

[14] Gordon W. Prange, with Donald M. Goldstein and Katherine V. Dillon, *Dec. 7, 1941: The Day the Japanese Attacked Pearl Harbor*, (New York: McGraw-Hill Book Company, 1988) 114.

[15] Ibid.

[16] Ibid.

remembered for his leadership and survivorship of December 7, 1941.

Cpl. Earl C. Nightingale

Twenty-year-old Marine Corporal Earl Nightingale hastily retreated from the mainmast of the *Arizona* and had no recollection of how he landed in the water. Once in the water, he thought he would be able to swim to Ford Island, but his arms and legs were in shock from the concussion of landing in the water, and Nightingale could not move. He thought he would drown, but fought the defeat with the thought of his youth and all he had to live for. His buddies cheered him on, but it was the strength of Major Shapely that helped Nightingale reach land. He told Nightingale, "Put your arms on my shoulders, and don't struggle or I'll bang you!"[17]

Bombs continued to pellet the water and during that time Nightingale and Shapely were separated by the constant wrenching of nausea that Shapely felt from the concussion of the bombs. Nightingale saluted as they both went under for what they thought would be their final time, yet that was not to be. They resurfaced and eventually reached their destination of Ford Island where they were met by hundreds of men who were charred beyond recognition and walking around in shock.

Nightingale witnessed the sinking of the *Arizona* and over 1,000 of his ship's mates from the shore that became his sanctuary that day.

---

[17] Ibid. 143.

Mark Ferris

Mark Ferris was blown out of his bunk as the first bombs started falling over Pearl Harbor on December 7, 1941. He was assigned to the 72nd bombardment squadron of the Army Air Corps at Hickam Field. Ferris survived the attack, but that date would change his life.

Fifteen years after the 'Day of Infamy,' Mr. Ferris was a manager at a California newspaper when he decided to see if America remembered Pearl Harbor. He was shocked when he sent an editor out to the streets to interview people about what happened on December 7, 1941, and learned that no one knew the significance of the date. At that point Ferris decided to form an organized group of Pearl Harbor survivors to lead the effort to inform the American public about what happened on December 7, 1941. The goal of the organization was to preserve the date of the attack in the memories of all Americans.

During the 1990s, Mr. Ferris and the Pearl Harbor Survivors Association heard about the World War II Memorial that Senator Bob Dole and Actor Tom Hanks were actively pursuing and they raised over $40,000 for the memorial. Since Mr. Ferris worked at Wal-Mart as a greeter during this time, he was able to gain donations from the Wal-Mart's World War II Memorial Fund drive that raised $14,500,000. Upon completion of the memorial, there were still over 25,000 Pearl Harbor survivors.

Because of the necessity on the part of Mark Ferris to remind America about what took place on December 7, 1941, the date is well known, and we will remember.

The motto of their group speaks volumes; it is "Remember Pearl Harbor—Keep America Alert—Eternal Vigilance is the Price of Liberty."[18]

---

[18] Online at www.pearlharborsurvivorsonline.org.

———

  The world would be a different place if America had continued their detachment and refrained from entering World War II. With the loss of so many lives on December 7, America stepped up to the plate and wrote the next several chapters of history for all the nations that we helped liberate. Once again, the sacrifice was great while freedom was maintained and, unfortunately, it all started on one day.

Chapter 4
September 11, 2001—America Terrorized

You can be sure that the American spirit will prevail over this tragedy.
—Colin Powell

AMERICANS ARE STILL REELING FROM the pain and trauma wrought to the bustling financial district of New York City and at our center of defense at the Pentagon. The pain, fear, panic and doom felt by each American on that day cannot be sufficiently described, because we felt our hearts sinking as the events of the day were reported. The skies were blue and it was a picture-perfect morning hosting calm serenity within the targeted sites. Like December 7, 1941, the innocence of the American mind and the wondrous untouchable and unstoppable spirit of a complete carefree attitude had a reality check. Just as a beautiful and ordinary day started on December 7, 1941, so it was on September 11, 2001. We were three months shy of 60 years since being severely threatened on our own territory.

Individuals who were alive on December 7, 1941, remember what they were doing when they received word that war had been waged and lives lost on the balmy shores of Hawaii. National crisis points make remarkable imprints on our lives and leave scars that are never blotted from memory. When September 11 claimed the innocent lives of Americans and several other nationalities, we grieved nationally, and the national grief for many of us extended to individuals from every walk of life and every ethnic group. From the Wall Street financiers, to the policemen, firefighters, window washers, restaurant owners, top military personnel and vacationers flying to a destination of relaxation, visitation and rest. The grieving resounded across America where the decimation and trauma were felt.

Although political battles are always being fought in the U.S. Capitol, this day the legislators from all political backgrounds came together and sang "God Bless America" on the Capitol steps the very afternoon we had been attacked. Their love for their country was far greater than any policy they disputed. Their determination set the precedence for the following days and months of grieving. Their call upon God to bless the land rang in every American heart.

Rudolph Giuliani

Mayor Giuliani had started his day early and was on his way to City Hall when he received the news that a plane had hit the World Trade Center. He immediately went to the site, which he later described as "the most horrific scene I've ever seen in my whole life."[19]

No other mayor in the history of America had been faced with the paramount travesty that occurred in New York, and Mayor Giuliani thrust himself into the middle of the effort of figuring out what was happening with steadiness, purpose and relentlessness. As thousands of people were fleeing the city, Mayor Giuliani walked among the rubble in his soiled clothes with a handkerchief covering his face trying to get as close to the scene as possible. His terror was replaced by anguish for the beloved Americans who had lost their lives.

The tragedy brought out his true ability to lead in such a time of crisis. He calmed New Yorkers and Americans and

---

[19] CBS News, *What We Saw,* (New York: Simon & Schuster, 2002), 100.

spread a positive message of hope and peace. September 11 birthed a new era to a politician who had spent much of his term as mayor trying to turn New York City around amidst controversy.

George W. Bush

Up to September 11, 2001, President George W. Bush had been dubbed as unsure and un-presidential by the media and those who had voted against him in the 2000 election. That all changed with this date, the President reassured the country many times over in the hours, days, weeks and months following the disaster that America had been hurt but not destroyed.

When the terrorism was being acted out that morning, President Bush was in Florida reading to school children and promoting literacy. As the events of the morning unfolded, the President was whisked out of sight by the Secret Service.

As we Americans sat glued to our television sets listening and watching the catastrophic events, newscasters were wondering aloud, "Where is the President?" and having full discussions with analysts and experts as to why the President was not visible. For me, I was glad I did not know where the President was, it meant he was being protected and that hopefully the terrorists would not be able to locate him. On September 11, 2001, we, as a nation, did not know exactly what was happening and where next we would be attacked. During such a crisis point, it was comforting to know that our intelligence, secret service and military operations were working tremendously hard and fast at discovering what exactly was taking place. It was comforting to see that our leaders were being cared for and protected. Without leadership, things would have become even more chaotic.

President Bush addressed the nation from the White House on the evening of September 11 and grieved with each family who had lost loved ones. Those who questioned his capability up to that date were amazed at the strength and collective determination the President displayed, and those who had faith in President Bush from the beginning were proud.

In the days that followed, the President was visible and outspoken. Perhaps the most effective and memorable phrase after the attacks was in New York City on September 14 where he stood among the rubble with the firefighters and shouted in a handheld megaphone "I can hear you. The rest of the world hears you. And the people who knocked these buildings down will hear all of us soon."[20]

President Bush had been in office for less than seven months when terrorism struck America. It would be the official beginning of an incredible presidency of a man who took the office he held seriously and without trepidation.

Joe Choti

An executive with MLB.com (Major League Baseball) located in a building several blocks from the World Trade Center, Joe usually arrived at the World Trade Center Station at 9 a.m., except on September 11. When I phoned his home early September 12, I was fearful of where he was. He answered the phone and I breathed a sigh of relief as I heard his voice. I told him I was thrilled to hear his voice, and I could hear his relief when he told me how he came to be at home.

"Can you believe it! I didn't go to the office yesterday because my brother-in-law's father passed away and we were at the funeral."[21]

Joe's wife, Kyra, and I had become friends when our

---

[20] David Frum, *The Right Man: The Surprise Presidency of George W. Bush*, (New York: Random House, 2003), 140.
[21] A personal conversation with Joe Choti, September 12, 2001.

daughters were in preschool together. She was grateful that her husband and her brother-in-law, who had a meeting scheduled in the WTC on the morning of September 11, were both not there that morning. In a way, her brother-in-law's father may have saved their lives by losing his own.

Jennifer Sands

As a pharmacist, Tuesdays were Jennifer's day off, and as she closed her eyes to sleep in a little later than usual, Jennifer heard her husband, Jim, prepare for his long commute into New York City. He usually left at 5:50 a.m. each morning, but on this particular day, she didn't receive her goodbye kiss until 6:05 a.m.—fifteen minutes late. They joked together at his lateness since they had been up until 1 a.m. watching the NY Giants Monday Night Football game. Jennifer heard Jim leave and silently prayed her daily prayer asking God for Jim's safe deliverance to work and safe return home.

Her last recollection of the early morning routine was, "I hear the garage door close and fall back to sleep."[22]

Jim was a strategic development engineer for eSpeed, a division of Cantor Fitzgerald. His office was on the 103rd floor of Tower One of the World Trade Center. As the morning's events unfolded, Jennifer paced in her kitchen, sat on the stairs and waited for word from Jim. Friends and family members were watching the attacks on television and moaned loudly when they saw Tower One collapse.

"I don't recall who said it. It doesn't matter. All I hear are the words, and I know it's all over: 'His tower collapsed,' someone says.

"And so did I."[23]

---

[22] Jennifer Sands, *A Tempered Faith: Rediscovering Hope in the Ashes of Loss*, (Savannah: The Olive Press, 2003), 4.

[23] Ibid., 16.

Dave Fontana

September 11 was a day of celebration for this firefighter. He and his wife, Marian, were spending the day together in commemoration of their eighth wedding anniversary. He had switched shifts so that he would have the day off to spend with his wife. After Marian dropped their son off at kindergarten, she headed toward Connecticut Muffin Shop, which was to be where she and Dave would connect and plan their day. The meeting never took place and the phone call that arranged their meeting was the last time the pair would speak. As a fireman, Dave was at the World Trade Center.

Marian's recollection conveys her feelings, "Sipping coffee I watched as a line of thick black smoke crept across the sky from Manhattan, oblivious to the fact that my life was about to change forever."[24]

She said that she knew the moment the South Tower fell that he was gone. "On a sunny September morning, the chord that connected my heart to Dave's was severed, ripped like a plug from its socket, and I knew he was gone."[25]

Lisa Beamer

Nothing about her name was known until the impact of what happened on United Flight 93 was learned. She was a young wife and mother of two small boys and expecting her third child. As she readied herself and her two sons to go grocery shopping on that Tuesday in September, she never made it. A phone call from her friend stopped her and propelled her to turn on the television. As she watched the events unfolding, she didn't realize that her husband, Todd Beamer, would be

---

[24] CBS News, *What We Saw*, (New York: Simon & Schuster, 2002), 56.
[25] Ibid., 63.

heralded as a hero of the flight and that he would be lost. Her life as an unknown homemaker in New Jersey was jolted into a wave of publicity and inspiration as she strongly testified to the world that her husband was in heaven.[26]

Jeremy Glick

Jeremy was booked on a flight to San Francisco out of Newark National Airport on Monday evening, September 10, 2001. When he arrived at the airport that evening, all flights were cancelled due to a fire on the runways, so he had to book a flight out of Newark on Tuesday morning. He was on United Flight 93 along with Todd Beamer and 35 other people. He left behind his wife, Liz, and their newborn daughter.

Tom Ridge

The governor of Pennsylvania had been on President Bush's list for cabinet appointments when the President was elected in 2000, but Tom Ridge was not chosen when the new President made his final selections. Whether there was disappointment or not, he continued his role as the popular governor of Pennsylvania. September 11, 2001, changed his aspirations, and his title as a new government office was established to protect our nation from future terrorist attacks. President George Bush was deliberate in his selection of Tom Ridge to be the new Director of Homeland Security.

---

[26] Lisa Beamer, *Let's Roll: Ordinary People, Extraordinary Courage,* (Wheaton, IL: Tyndale House Publishers, Inc.), 62.

The Pentagon

September 11, 1941, was the date that the Pentagon officially opened. Ironically 60 years later, the building was a target of terrorism. The arrogance of the terrorists to target our defense intelligence center AND the World Trade Center was more than anyone could have imagined. One year later, on September 11, 2002, the part of the Pentagon that had been hit by the airplane was repaired and reopened—a sign of America's resilience and that even though one date in time dramatically changed America, new breath and life were breathed into the historical defense landmark.

Although only a few names were mentioned in this section, we know that almost three thousand people lost their lives and every one of them had a story to tell. Each individual had specific dates and events leading up to September 11 that had put them in the unfortunate path of evil. I wish I could have written the story of all those who lost their lives, but that is not the purpose of this book. Even still, we know that their lives were changed on one day. Each person whose life was eternally altered on September 11, 2001, was going about life and living whether it was by going to work like every other day, or taking care of children, starting a vacation or traveling for business. Their lives were normal until one unforeseen moment in time. Nothing can quite prepare anyone for times of such tragic devastation.

September 11, 2001, left three physical craters in our nation—the Twin Towers, the Pentagon, and Shenksville, Pennsylvania—but the craters in the hearts of those who lost a loved one are felt far more and devastate anyone who could put themselves in the shoes of the lost. The date was an ordinary date that will forever be etched in the heart and spirit of America.

Summary of Part I

THE REASON THESE FOUR PARTICULAR days were chosen for research is because each of them took place on American soil. The loss of the lives of Americans in our own back yard due to war and in defense of freedom is near and dear to my heart for although my ancestry is from European descent, I am an American—not Irish, not Scottish, not Welch, or anything else but American. The soils that hold American blood are hallowed ground and represent the price that has been paid for the freedoms we enjoy. Without the Revolution and a Declaration of Independence, we'd be English citizens and the United States would not have existed. Without the Civil War, the United States would not be united and there would be two countries—a North and a South. Without Pearl Harbor, perhaps the USA could have held off a little longer from entering the war. However, what would have happened to the world without the intervention of America? Without September 11, 2001, many Americans would not be widows, orphans, or grieving parents, siblings and friends. Yes, freedom is expensive to claim. It's a price tag that will never know a number.

For each significant date that was studied, there were thousands of lives touched by one date in history. Many lives were lost and countless more were left to grieve those lost.

How do we get past the grief felt by a nation as a whole and individuals whose lives were dented and scarred? The price for living in America and being American is worth the cost. Fortunately our Founding Fathers, the Civil War and World War II heroes believed in the sovereignty of the United States of America. Without their courage, bravery and love for this country, we would not be celebrating freedom and living in a land of independence.

Part II
Momentous Dates of an Individual's Life

*To be what we are, and to become what we are capable
of becoming, is the only end of life.*
–Robert Louis Stevenson

OVER THE COURSE OF A lifetime there are decisions made
on our behalf and choices we make that will set the direction of
our life. Each day we are faced with choices that will be the
ultimate outcome of what will be. The person addicted to drugs
made a choice one day to experiment. The alcoholic took the
first drink. The list goes on about the choices we make, but our
destiny is not always determined by our choices, but by things
beyond our control.

The teenager who steps out after graduation often thinks
he's going to be different than the rest of his classmates. The
daughter may be determined not to be like her mother and the
son may dream of being like his father. Many times, we make
choices that do not coincide with our dreams so we begin the
path to a lesser-fulfilled life than we imagined at sixteen or
seventeen years old. But the choices that we make, many times
do determine where we end up, even though we may never
know the answers to many of our questions. The path we
choose is a result of choices that we made and also
circumstances beyond our control and those two things are
what makes the difference.

For every person whose existence was directly altered by

events that took place on July 4, 1776, July 3, 1863, December 7, 1941, or September 11, 2001, there were decisions that brought them to the place of distinction or vulnerability. The dates of those choice could have been life-changing events brought on by divine intervention and timing. Timing from events earlier in the individuals' lives.

Chapter 5
Graduation—Taking on the World

Education is learning what you didn't even know you didn't know.
                                                        –Daniel Boorstin

WHEN WE LOOK AT SIGNIFICANT DATES that shape our lives, graduation from high school or college may or may not be one of them. However, at that time between innocent young person to grounded adult, the date is significant. On that day in each of our lives, our future is set before us and we think we own it. Unfortunately real life steps in all too quickly and reminds us of our imperfect humanity and strips us of the confidence and zeal we had during those tender late teen and early twenties years.

After graduation, there are worlds to conquer, careers to get on with and changes to make. We are filled with dreams and goals of what we want to accomplish. Many achieve those goals and move on to bigger and better ambitions; however, it is easy to give up life's dreams and aspirations and become bogged down with life and forget those rainbow-colored desires. The dates below represent people who did not let their ideas fade away but who stayed the course of time.

June 20, 1940

After five years of studying at Harvard, Jack Kennedy graduated with a bachelor of Political Science degree cum laude. The young Kennedy was preparing himself for a political career and had already determined to enter Yale Law School in the fall of 1940. The date of his graduation from Harvard held even more importance as he was devoting much of his time and energy to finding a publisher for his senior thesis that became a best-selling book, *Why England Slept.* As a Kennedy, Jack was expected to attend only the finest of educational institutions and outshine the best, but the young man was not expected to excel to the degree of becoming the President of the United States; that was for his father or brother Joe to accomplish. However, we know from history that it is not always the expected person who gains the prize, but the least expected. JFK set himself on a course and he did so with great success.[27]

June 12, 1942

Not everyone graduates from high school, celebrates an eighteenth birthday and joins the Navy all in one day, but that is exactly what the 41st President of the United States did. His graduation day was remarkable in the fact that on June 12, 1942, our country and the world were in the midst of World War II and he was eager to get started in his quest to help the war effort and get on with life. That one day changed President George Bush's life in a significant way. He became the youngest pilot in the Navy in 1943 when he received his wings. His high-school graduation date was not planned around parties

---

[27] Nigel Hamilton, *JFK: Reckless Youth,* (New York: Random House, 1992), 328.

and friends, but around his future.

George H.W. Bush did not know on that date in 1942 that he would one day be the Vice President and President of the United States, but the date began his journey toward the future that may have been dramatically altered if a submarine hadn't rescued him after his plane was shot down in 1944.

A specific date in June 1942 was just the beginning of life filled with service to his country and family.[28]

June 10, 1958

Young Colin Powell had attended CCNY and became a part of the ROTC program while in college. On the evening of June 9, 1958, the Commissioning Ceremony took place for all ROTC participants. Each participant had to take the Officers' Oath to serve faithfully in the armed forces. For Colin Powell, it was the beginning of a lengthy and substantial military career that prepared him for the important posts he would serve as National Security Advisor to the President, Chairman of the Joint Chiefs of Staff and Secretary of State. The boy who spent his early years in Harlem overcame prejudice and became a respected national leader. His graduation day was just the beginning for the determined young man.[29]

These three men took significant steps in their lives to follow their dreams. A couple of them were from more fortunate backgrounds of substantial means, but there are far more people who are from ordinary families that head for extraordinary lives. Lives carved out by planning one day at a time and forging pathways to the future.

---

[28] Barbara Bush, *Barbara Bush: A Memoir,* (New York: Lisa Drew Books/Charles Scribner's Sons 1994), Page 18.
[29] Colin Powell, *My American Journey*, (New York: Random House, 1995), 36.

Instead of getting down on ourselves about the choices we have made since our high school and college graduations, we should look over our lives and the choices we have made and celebrate the life that we have lived so far. We should reflect and bask in knowing that those choices and decisions have molded us into who we are. Sometimes the pathway may not have been at all what we planned for ourselves, but we can overcome the wrong that we have done or the disappointments we have had and draw from the mistakes to make more pleasing choices in the future. The particular day of graduation was just the beginning of what was to come. That one day was a gateway through the path to the rest of our lives. It is vital to celebrate those gates.

Many times I think about the decisions that I made in my late teens and early twenties and wish I could go back and change them. I think that if I just could have thought through things with a more discerning and mature mind that maybe I would have accomplished much more than I have. Even though I think like that, I also know that I would not be where I am or even who I am without making those less mature decisions at such a young age. These regrets are natural, but we should never wallow in self-pity because it will only lead to a destructive road. Those regrets may be what Garth Brooks sang about in his song, "Unanswered Prayers." In the song, the man has his wife beside him when he meets up with his high-school sweetheart, who he used to pray to marry. But as he looks at his wife, he's glad that the high-school prayer was never answered, because he would not have married his wife. The song portrays how what we think we want is not really what we want and not what we should have.

As we grow older, we can always look back at our younger days and wish for differences, but even if we could go back and change, would we? Because each decision is a part of another decision and it becomes a domino effect. If you had not graduated from that particular college, you would not have met your best friend who you are now seeing through a difficult divorce. If you had not attended a certain school, you would not have married your spouse when you did, and you would not be planning your daughter's 16th birthday party. Whatever the case may be, the day you graduated, in a sense, changed your life forever. The gate you went through mapped the road you are on now. The *Unanswered Prayers* may have actually been God's answer, and it was "No."

Chapter 6
Wedding Day

If you deny yourself commitment, what can you do with your life?
—Harvey Fierstein

A WEDDING DAY IS NOT only one of the biggest days of the lives of a man and woman who come together to pledge a lasting commitment, but it is also one of the biggest decisions two people make. Later in the book we will look into another big day and decision made on an individual basis; however, right now let's focus on the magnitude of the sacredness of matrimony.

Weddings come in all sizes and costs. Some people quietly rendezvous and get married with a couple of witnesses and a preacher or justice of the peace. The cost is less than $100 depending on the state with which the marriage license is purchased. Other weddings cost thousands and even millions of dollars with hundreds and thousands of guests to witness the nuptials and wish the happy couple a wonderful life. Still other couples fly off to exotic tropical locations to have the romantic dream of a lifetime to exchange their vows.

Regardless of where a couple marries, the union is still the same. The place, the cost, or those in attendance are insignificant in the scope of marriage. The wedding day is sacred and a date of remembrance for the bride and groom no matter the time in planning or the cost or the guest list.

Let's talk about the planning. The average couple takes at

least 12 months to plan their wedding day. Many couples are on the long-term plan where they plan their wedding day for two or three years! There are many reasons couples delay the plans, and that is irrelevant to the point; however, why does it seem more people put so much time, preparation and money into planning for the "biggest event" of their life, and yet spend so little time in pre-marital counseling? Engaged couples spend exorbitant amounts of money, exhaustive amounts of time, and go through many disagreements and family feuds before they even exchange their vows. The preparation for the wedding seems to be more important than actually planning the marriage.

A wedding day is such a tremendous day in life, but not because of the guests and the food and the cake, but because of the commitment that two people are making. Two people are coming together *forever* to promise to love each other. This is massive! Yet marriage is taken lightly and is, unfortunately, so easy to dispose of. If more couples contemplated the severity of the commitment, maybe less mistakes would be made, perhaps less divorces would be filed, thus fewer children would be affected by broken homes. This ONE day makes a decisive difference in more than just one life.

Think back to the day that you and your spouse came together and consecrated your lives as a unified family. Maybe it's time to dust off the wedding album or rewind the videotape and reflect on the part of your life that began that day. None of us really have a clue what we are doing when we get married, unless, of course, we have been through marriage before. But for that first-time marriage, the love is so full of passion and excitement that we cannot fathom the road that lies ahead of us.

Weddings generate couples, which generate children, which generate families, which generate generations based on *one* day in the life of two people. Two people come together to form a committed bond that will not just affect the two of them, but will affect their families, their parents and their siblings because there is now an extended family unit in place. There

50

are holidays celebrated together, family parties, and sad times shared with at least two different families.

When two people exchange those vows and sign the marriage license, their world has changed and the affects of those changes will be evident in the hours, days, weeks, months and years to come. Children are produced in most marriages, which then should bind the couple further together, but as we often see, half of all marriages fail through the course of time. This book is not about the whys and wherefores of weddings and the divorce rate. The point is that the wedding day between two people changes the course of many lives for generations. Therefore, that *one day* changes two peoples' lives forever, and the effects of that decision is felt by more than just those two people.

November 1773

Young independent Betsy Griscom left her Quaker tradition at the opposition of her parents to become the wife of an Episcopalian, John Ross. Her negligence to repent for having married outside her faith had her excommunicated from the Quakers and forced much ridicule and grief on her parents. Her parents would not intimidate the young bride, when her new groom took her to their small brick home on Arch Street in Philadelphia. It was at this home, the young Betsy Ross would encounter three guests: her father-in-law, Colonel George Ross; Statesman Robert Morris; and General George Washington, who came to acquire her services for making the first American Flag, The Stars and Stripes. It is remarkable to think that her mark in history was made at the home where John Ross brought his bride one November night before our country was even independent.[30]

---

[30] Edwin S. Parry, *Betsy Ross: Quaker Rebel*, (Philadelphia: The John C. Winston Company, 1932), 40.

June 12, 1806

This date was the beginning of a new life for young Thomas Lincoln and his bride, Nancy Hanks. The uneducated pair had both come from unremarkable backgrounds and worked hard to make a living. After their marriage, they moved several times over the course of a few years. Their marriage produced three children, one of which died in infancy, but their second born would grow into a popular President of the United States. The Lincolns' marriage was spent moving and resettling in different places and their union was abruptly ended when Nancy died in October 1818 from a disease called "milk sickness."

The union of two ordinary people on June 12, 1806, reshaped American History and brought forth the 16th President of the United States.[31]

February 1, 1916

Grace Episcopal Church in Grand Rapids, Michigan, was the scene where two young people met at a church social and it was the scene for their wedding in 1916. Twenty-four-year-old Gerald Ford and single mother, Dorothy Gardner King, started their lives together as a threesome with Dorothy's two-year-old son, Leslie Lynch King, Jr. Leslie was transformed that day into Gerald Rudolph Ford Jr. to remove all traces of an abusive father that the boy would never have a relationship with. For little "Junie" Ford this day marked the transformation of a notorious life and a loving relationship with the father who adopted him the day the man married his mother. Gerald Ford became the 38th President of the United States. A less than

---

[31] Carl Sandburg, *Abe Lincoln Grows Up*, (New York: Harcourt, Brace & World, Inc., 1956), 29.

significant date for the majority changed the destiny of one little boy and his mother.[32]

June 30, 1916

Virginia Leftwich and Nelson Bell were married and started their new life together in the coal fields of West Virginia, where the young medical practitioner served residency. The couple eventually became missionaries in China. The Bells' second daughter, Ruth, would one day marry a famous evangelist. The marriage that brought about one such Ruth Bell Graham, gave Billy Graham his lifelong partner.[33]

January 8, 1956

It was a cold and wintry day in the little village of Tioga Center, New York, but that didn't stop the bride and groom from being at the church on time. They had a church full of family and friends awaiting their big moment, and the weather did not alter their plans. The groom's father, Reverend Walter Garrison, joined Wendell Garrison and Ruth Best together in holy matrimony. Their union bore five children and lasts to this day, although upset by the onset of Alzheimer's disease that has robbed Ruth from enjoying her grandchildren and Wendell's retirement. Their fourth child and youngest daughter is me, and I would not be writing this book if not for that date.

Establishing the significance of ordinary dates and noting important dates is what life is about. The best thing for young couples to recognize as they determine to commit themselves

---

[32] Bonnie Angelo, *First Mothers: The Women Who Shaped The Presidents*, (New York: Harper Collins, 2000), 234.

[33] Patricia Cornwell, *Ruth: A Portrait* (New York: Doubleday, 1997), 15.

to each other is to focus on what a commitment of marriage means in the whole scheme of life. It's not just the wedding date that changes lives; it's the commitment that will affect the following generations.

Chapter 7
Birth Days

Just when I think I have learned the way to live, life changes.
—Hugh Prather

IT HAS BEEN A LONG NINE months for the woman. She feels as big as a house, as crabby as a crab, as sick as a dog, and fed up to her gills with being pregnant. But that first time mother is worried that she will not know what a contraction is, and she is so uncomfortable that she is sure that the torture cannot get worse. She actually has come to a point of wondering if there really is going to be a baby born. But, oh, the contractions begin, and there is no turning back because that baby is definitely coming. It's during those moments (hours for some) of hard labor that the woman is actually thinking of sending the baby back and leaving it in the womb because she cannot endure another contraction.

Then those first soft muffled squeaks are heard, and the labor is over. The next emotion is often one of joy. The painful contractions have subsided and there is this tiny little infant that the doctors and nurses hand to the woman before the baby is even cleaned off. The happy parents enjoy those first few seconds after birth until the lungs of the new infant are at full throttle, then things really become interesting. But those first few seconds of the actual birth are priceless pieces of time that will never leave their memory banks, because in those seconds the parents are flooded with more emotions than they ever thought possible. They often feel complete joy at the beautiful miracle of new life, and pride at the resemblance of the union of the parents. That day is *one day* that will change three lives forever: the mother, the father, and the person that has just entered the world. That day will be celebrated yearly until death. What an abundant day.

The day of childbirth marks the beginning of parenthood and marks a point in time of a new person. It is an added responsibility for the parents and a new personality in the world. If there are more children that follow, their birthdays are just as significant. Whenever, there is new life, there are additional responsibilities and increased demands. Through the years more memories are built on the birth of each child, and there are more dates with which to celebrate the priceless gift of living. That is why every year is marked and celebrated on one specific day, because that day made a big difference in the makeup of one family.

February 11, 1732

(Later became February 22, when England adopted the Gregorian calendar.)

Mary Ball Washington was of normal status and considered an ordinary woman when she gave birth to her firstborn son on February 11, 1732. She could not have known the greatness that her son would achieve when she cuddled him to her that day. As she held the tiny bundle and touched his fingers and toes, how was she to know that he would be extraordinary? As the second wife of Augustine Washington, who had children from his first marriage, Mary's first child was born only eleven months after their marriage. George Washington's birthplace was a four-room home in Popes Creek, Virginia.[34]

We still commemorate Washington's birthday and recognize it with Abraham Lincoln's as important dates to remember. The significant events that came from Washington's birth date are too numerous to mention in this book. Let's just say, he was the "Father of our Nation" and his name is the name of many towns, cities, monuments and sites across America. We could say that February 11, 1732, was the beginning of what our nation became. That one day was momentous.

May 20, 1782

A different kind of birth took place for Robert Shurtliff, a young soldier for the Continental Army during the Revolutionary War. He was born in Worcester, Massachusetts, at an Army enlistment facility. He was not a baby, but a woman. Deborah Sampson had long wanted to be a warrior for the Revolutionary cause, but because she was a woman, she knew that her time would never come—or would it? Deborah embarked on secretly changing her identity to become the only woman to fight in the Revolutionary War as Robert Shurtliff. She took the name from the first and middle name of her oldest brother who had died at the age of eight prior to her birth.

Deborah encountered all that soldiers endured and retained her secret until a near-death bout with malaria revealed the truth to the surgeon examining her. The surgeon kept her secret while she recuperated, but she was given an honorable discharge once the truth was known. Robert Shurtliff ended her military career and became Deborah Sampson once again.[35]

---

[34] George Washington, *A Biography in His Own Words,* (New York: Newsweek Book Division, 1972), 16.

[35] Lucy Freeman and Alma Bond, Ph.D., *America's First Woman Warrior*, (New York: Paragon House, 1992).

February 12, 1809

A baby boy was born to ordinary people in a small log cabin in Kentucky. His parents, Nancy and Thomas, named him Abraham. The Lincolns were hard-working people with very little, if any, education. The date the baby was born would not be significant to anybody but them for many years, but Abraham Lincoln overcame the difficulties of an uneducated childhood to become one of America's most respected presidents. Abraham lost his mother to disease when he was nine years old. His father was unable to keep the household and eventually married a woman who had great influence on the future president. Sarah Bush Johnston, Abraham's stepmother, brought order to his life and saw to it that Abraham received enough education to read and write—it amounted to less than a year of schooling. However, the education he received was enough to arouse a desire to learn and Abraham traveled all over the Indiana countryside borrowing books.

Lincoln's life started ordinarily and ended extraordinarily, which shows what determination and the will to succeed can do. We still celebrate the birth of this remarkable man and salute the courage that enabled him to beat the odds to abolish slavery and maintain the union.

December 25, 1821

A welcoming Christmas present came to the home of Stephen and Sara Barton in 1821. The couple welcomed their newborn daughter to their home in North Oxford, Massachusetts. They named their fifth child, Clarissa Harlowe Barton, a.k.a. Clara Barton. The young girl would grow up to be referred to as the "Angel of the Battlefield" during the Civil War and also would establish the American Red Cross. Clara Barton was just another baby in 1821, but by April 1912, in her ninetieth year, her life history of helping others every step of the way was long and selfless. She had touched many in her pursuit to make life as comfortable as possible for every individual she encountered and took after her father's initiative to note the importance of being educated as she taught countless individuals from every age group. This was no ordinary date or just another Christmas in North Oxford, Massachusetts, but the date that a "True Heroine of the Age" was born.[36]

November 10, 1919

Jarabenia, Czechoslovakia, was the birthplace for Mychal Strenk, son of Vasil and Martha. Mychal came into the world and lived in a one-room house with a dirt floor, along with his father's parents and grandparents. His parents were probably like other parents with the birth of their first child, yet would they have any idea the momentous role their son would play? They had no way of knowing how their decision to immigrate to America would change the course for their son. Mychal Strenk immigrated to America with his mother in 1922 to join his father, who had immigrated in 1920. Vasil had changed the family's name to Strank and somewhere along the line Mychal became Mike.

Mike joined the Marines on October 6, 1939, long before he would have been drafted. He wished to join after his application for an extension with the Civilian Conservation Corps (CCC) was not granted. At nineteen years old, Mike had grown and matured and had been well trained for service.

Far from the quietness of Franklin Borough, Pennsylvania, where he grew up, Mike Strank was a Marine Corporal stationed at New River, North Carolina (now known as Camp

---

[36] Candice Ransom, *Clara Barton,* (Minneapolis: Lerner Publications Company, 2003), 6.

Lejeune), with Company K when America was pulled into war on December 7, 1941.

Mike became a sergeant and was assigned to Company E, known as Easy Company by his battalion. He and his unit were a tight band who had fought together throughout many vicious battles. Mike was one of the brave men who raised the flag on Iowa Jima along with five other soldiers from his company. He became known nationally by the publicized picture but was not allowed the fame that came from that picture; because eight days after the snapshot was taken, Mike made the ultimate sacrifice on Iowa Jima. As he was drawing an escape route for his men, an explosion killed him.

James Bradley described the scene in his book, *Flags of Our Fathers*.

"Almost certainly, the round had come from a U.S. destroyer offshore; it sliced through the only unprotected side of the outcropping. The Czech immigrant to America, born on the Marine Corps birthday, serving his third tour of duty for his adopted country, the sergeant who was a friend to his boys, was cut down by friendly fire."[37]

The significance of his life was awarded a purple heart and a host of other medals and awards. The most important thing about Mike was his loyalty and concern for those in his charge, and that's what his life and leadership were about. November 10, 1919, was a very significant day because of the birth of Mike Strank.

---

[37] James Bradley, *Flags of Our Fathers*, (New York: Bantam Books, 2000), 231.

March 26, 1930

A little girl was born in El Paso, Texas, to cattle ranchers in a home without electricity or running water. Branding steer and fixing broken equipment around the family's Lazy B Ranch were common tasks that the bright young Sandra Day was a part of during her childhood. Because of the lack of quality education for a young girl in Arizona, Sandra was sent to live with her grandmother in El Paso, Texas, to attend a private school for girls and then Austin High. Upon her high-school graduation, Sandra went on to attend Stanford University and graduated *magna cum laude* in 1950 with a bachelor's degree in Economics. Two years later she completed Stanford Law School and started her journey toward the highest court in the land. After her graduation from law school, Sandra married fellow law student, John O'Connor, and her name was changed to Sandra Day O'Connor. The ranch girl from Arizona paved the way for young girls and women, not as a feminist, but as a committed American woman who excelled on her merit, qualifications, and determination all the way to the Supreme Court.[38]

Everyone has a date that marked their entrance to humanity. A birthday is one momentous day for every human being born. Although some births are short lived and others long celebrated, there is always something to rejoice about when a new life breathes its first breath. There is purpose to every human, and it starts with the day they were born.

---

[38] Sandra Day O'Connor and H. Alan Day, *Lazy B: Growing Up on a Cattle Ranch in the American Southwest,* (New York: Random House, 2002).

Chapter 8
Life-threatening Moments

We poison our lives with fear of burglary and shipwreck and...the house is never burgled, and the ship never goes down.
                                                            –Jean Anouilh

HOPEFULLY, MOST OF US LIVE life every day outside of worrying about what could happen or what might happen. Life cannot truly be lived if one is constantly fretting over the things that could—but most likely will never occur. Living in fear of the unknown is halting to the very existence of a person. People who live in a constant state of worry are robbing themselves of the joy that living can bring. There is a time and place for caution and concern to be demonstrated; yet to worry about what may never happen causes more stress than necessary and only devalues your life. If and when illness strikes, there is a sense of panic and fear that is only natural, but such times can also be blessings in disguise.

Unfortunately as much as life is a gift, we know that it can be taken at any given moment in time on any day. We are reminded daily of the fragility of life when we read the obituaries and find that not everyone is "old" when they die. Life may be taken when we least expect it, thus living in a state of panic is not the answer to life-threatening moments. It is those moments that give courage and strength to a person and family where they thought they had none. The fight for life is in all of us. It is something we are born with, so we will fight for every breath to maintain what we know on earth as life. Day after day, however, we are reminded of the fragileness of our lives, which is why it is so important to live each day to the fullest. Enjoying those moments and doing what we love to do is what is important. Working to have more material possessions is not what you would do if you knew you had six months to live.

There are those few that are faced with tragic and disheartening circumstances that look at life with a whole new set of glasses on because they were given a second chance at life and they recognize how important that is. On this earth, we are only given one chance to live, but for a few, they get another chance to live it.

March 30, 1981

The Washington Hilton was one mile from the White House and was the site for a meeting of the Construction Trades Council. Recently inaugurated, President Ronald Reagan was slated to speak to the group and then return to the White House. After giving his speech, he and his entourage left through a side entrance to get into his waiting car. A reporter yelled a question for the President. As the President turned toward the reporter, a member of the Secret Service instead guided the President toward the waiting car with one hand and with the other hand pushed the Press Secretary, James Brady, toward the shouting reporter. Within five seconds mayhem broke loose and four men had been shot by six gunshots. James Brady had been shot in the left temple and the devastation of the bullet scarred him for life. Thomas Delehanty, a district patrolman, was shot in the neck, and Secret Service agent Tim McCarthy stood with his arms outstretched between the bullet and the President and took a bullet in the chest.

At first, it did not seem like the President had been shot so the motorcade was heading for the White House, until Jerry

Parr noticed the President coughing blood into a cloth. They whisked the President to George Washington University Hospital where after a few examinations, they finally found the entrance wound under his arm. When they surgically removed the bullet, they found that it had torn through the President's lung and stopped one inch away from his heart.

Ronald Reagan knew his life had been spared that day and that because of the difference in height between James Brady and President Reagan, the bullet that hit Brady in the head would have hit President Reagan's heart and killed him.

Secret Service agent Mike Deaver recalls a conversation he had with the President shortly after the incident:

> He felt the Lord had spared him to fulfill whatever mission it was that he was supposed to fulfill. And he was gonna make sure that he lived his life to the fullest and did whatever he considered to be the right thing for the rest of his life.[39]

Ronald Reagan had been the President for just nine weeks when one event changed everything. Three other lives were physically scarred from the bullets they received on that date. Four people were given a second chance when five seconds marred them for life. James Brady never recovered fully, but he and his wife have become two of the most prominent gun control advocates.

---

[39] Peggy Noonan, *When Character Was King*, (New York: Penguin Putnam, Inc., 2001), 194.

October 2, 1996

Lance Armstrong told in his book, *It's Not About the Bike: My Journey Back to Life*, how he left his house one day as one person, but when he arrived home later that night he was another. In one day his life drastically changed. He learned that he had testicular cancer at the age of 25 and it had metastasized to his lungs. This meant he had Stage III cancer and would be undergoing surgery and aggressive chemotherapy treatments. The thriving young cyclist realized that he was in the battle for his life and that he may never compete or ride again.

He explained the fear that he felt; "I thought I knew what fear was, until I heard the words *you have cancer*."[40]

He strongly fought and defeated cancer and then went back to competing. Not only had he beaten the deadly disease, but he went on to win the Tour de France.

> Cancer forced me to develop a plan for living, and that, in turn, taught me how to develop a plan for smaller goals like each stage of the Tour. It also taught me how to cope with losing. It taught me that sometimes the experience of losing things, whether health or a home or an old sense of self, has its own value in the scheme of life.[41]

May 27, 1995

The questions of what happened and how the events unfolded will most likely be with Christopher Reeve as he relives the few seconds that altered his body in a way that would never be the same. His horse, Buck, stopped short of a jump in a Memorial Day horse show competition that caused

---

[40] Lance Armstrong, *It's Not About the Bike; My Journey Back to Life,* (New York: The Berkley Publishing Group, 2000), 70.
[41] Ibid., 284.

Christopher to flip headfirst over Buck and land on his head. The accident was instantaneous and unpreventable for the skilled equestrian, but he still wonders if he had sat differently on the saddle, whether the outcome would have been different. He wonders if his hands had not been tangled in the bridle so tightly if just his wrist would have been broken instead of two vertebrae. Regardless, in an instant his life drastically changed. Not only his life was changed that day, but the lives of his wife, Dana and their two-year-old son, Will. The day that changed his life happened suddenly, without previous warning and it would change his lifestyle and that of his family's forever. Although he survived the near-death experience, he is a paraplegic.[42]

January 8, 2002

Six busy weeks led up to this date. I was holding our crying 17-month-old, Justin, as green goop poured out of his nose; helping our six-year-old, Tyler, with schoolwork and wondering why our four-year old daughter, Lexi, was still in bed asleep at 10 o'clock in the morning. I answered the ringing phone and placed it on my shoulder so I could still do things with my free hand. It was an office worker from my surgeon's office asking if I could see a Dr. Middini* at one o'clock that afternoon. On January 3 I had surgery to remove a lump in my breast that the surgeon reassured me was nothing more than a cyst. I didn't understand the call, and was anxious to speak with my surgeon, but she was in surgery and would call me as soon as she was free. I hung up from the phone call confused. I grabbed the Yellow Pages and looked up the physician reference for Dr. Middini to see what kind of doctor he was. The advertisement for his practice read, "Excellence in cancer care."

---

[42] Christopher Reeve, *Still Me*, (New York: Random House, Inc., 1998), 17-20.

That was how I found out I had breast cancer. The day started as a normal day and ended in the battle for my life. That day changed my life and made me understand what a second chance was.

I am convinced that before breast cancer, I lived my life in a state of 'cruise control' unaware of the bump that lay ahead in the road. The jolt from the bump moved me out of the passing lane and onto the shoulder to a place where I was forced to stop and wait. Although at times the waiting was painful, I am grateful to be one of the many survivors of cancer. Fortunately for me, the events surrounding January 8, 2002, were a blessing because of the medical research and skilled physicians and surgeons, I was given a fighting chance at life.

Millions of people struggle with life-threatening diagnosis and diseases and the frightening aspects are overwhelming, but with each day there is a need to fight and cling to the life that we know. Just as I was shocked to be a victim of cancer, so you or someone you are close to may one day face the same ton of bricks as they hear the words "You have...." You fill in the blank. There is a devastation that comes with any disease that threatens your life, but it does not have to crush your spirit and rob you of your love of life because you have the opportunity to realize that life is worth fighting for and that each day is a building block of living.

Famous author and motivational speaker Og Mandino said:

> I am convinced that many times, in the course of our lives, God challenges us with a golden opportunity, a seemingly impossible hurdle, or a terrible tragedy...and how we react or *fail* to react—determines the course of our future, almost as if we were involved in some sort of heavenly chess game...with our destiny always in balance.[43]

---

[43] Og Mandino, *A Better Way to Live* (New York: Bantam, 1990), 6-7.

ESTHER HUGHES

This quote sets the tone for how grateful we should be that we are not in as much control of our lives or our destiny as we might think. There is someone who controls what goes on in this world, and we are the players for a greater cause.

President Ronald Reagan recovered from his wound and went on to write eight years of history as the 40th President of the United States of America. Lance Armstrong fought and won his battle with cancer and trained harder and became more determined, which allowed him to become the heroic winner of the Tour de France. Christopher Reeve could have become a recluse because of the paraplegic state his unfortunate accident left him, but instead he founded the Christopher Reeve Paralysis Foundation. His foundation provides funding for research to find cures for paralysis caused by spinal cord injuries and other central nervous system disorders. The foundation also provides grants and other resources for people with paralysis related disabilities.

All of these men could have wallowed in self-pity for their circumstances and given up their chance at living a fulfilled life, but they each met the situation head-on and turned a tragedy into a way of serving others. Those of us who have been given a second chance should have a great sense of gratitude for the blessing in living because having faced death at a time when we were living high brought us to the point of relinquishing control and knowing that life is a vapor just as the wise King Solomon proclaimed.

68

Chapter 9
Death–Loss of a Loved One

What is your life? You are a mist that appears for a little while and then vanishes.

(James 4:14, NIV)

EVERY DAY NEWSPAPERS TELL THE story of a person's life in the obituaries. Although we may educate ourselves to know the date that some famous person died, we, who have no emotional ties to that person, do not mourn the loss. We mourn the loss of those closest to us and of those that live during our generation. Physical death is guaranteed to each individual that is conceived. The minute life starts so the days get closer to departing the earth, which is why each day should be a celebration of life.

Whether a loved one loses their life to a long illness or a sudden blow, death is still the final string that breaks us apart from the world. When a young child is taken from this life, he or she leaves behind overwhelming grief and loss to its parents and siblings. When a young adult dies, it is a sorrowful time as family members cannot help but question what would have been if that person had been allowed a full life. When a parent dies, children are left behind missing their biggest link to childhood and the security that loving and stable parents bring to the family unit. When grandparents die, they leave behind a hole that only a grandmother or grandfather can fill in a child's world. With each loss, there is grief and heartache sets in. A life has been halted and those left behind are jolted into a reality check and a reminder that life is fleeting.

There are also always unanswered questions whether it is from the standpoint of why this person's life was taken in that way, or the standpoint of never knowing the innermost thoughts of the person who has passed away.

The world turns every day and lives are changed instantly. Is there something you would like to be remembered by?

January 21, 1776

The occurrence of a gunpowder explosion took the life of young John Ross before he ever had the chance to fight in a battle of the Revolution as a part of the Pennsylvania Militia. His life was suddenly halted as his wife, Betsy, optimistically waited and worked from their home hoping for a quick end to the war. The young wife tried to nurse her broken husband back to health, but without any success. Her world was shattered on the cold snowy day as she prepared the lifeless body of her husband for burial. He did not live to greet the three visitors who would come to his home and meet with his wife in a few short months. He never knew the historical figure his wife would become by the crafting of the first Stars and Stripes. To this day the house that he and his bride shared is a historical monument of the founding of our country. He never knew the fame of that tiny little home in Philadelphia because his life was snuffed out in an instant.[44]

---

[44] Edwin S. Parry, *Betsy Ross: Quaker Rebel*, (Philadelphia: The John C. Winston Company, 1932), 72-74.

July 12, 1804

History recorded what happened on July 11, 1804, but unfortunately some of the details were left out as Aaron Burr and Alexander Hamilton made their way across the Hudson River to Weehawken, New Jersey. The two statesmen had long disliked each other and disagreed with one another, but to take it to the level of dueling was not necessary. That did not stop them from their ignorant quest. The two met and the rest is history, or so it seems. Even though the historic account of what happened that morning could not be 100 percent proven because the four witnesses did not actually see the shots fired because they were obeying the rules of dueling (*code duello*). Burr was the challenger, however, and Hamilton was the loser because the bullet he took above the hip ricocheted off his rib and paved its way through the liver and diaphragm. He did not die instantly, but lived long enough to be surrounded by his doctor, the Episcopalian Bishop from New York, and his wife and seven children. The decision he made to face Aaron Burr left him dead. Although Burr was the "winner," he never emotionally or psychologically recovered from the dueling event that left Hamilton's children fatherless.[45]

July 4, 1826

Fifty years after *The Declaration of Independence* was signed and the date the United States celebrated its birth, two of our Founding Fathers passed away just hours apart. Thomas Jefferson and John Adams passed from this earth on the same date. Both men had played an important role in the blueprints of our nation, and both served as Presidents. As the fiftieth

---

[45] Richard Brookhiser, *Alexander Hamilton: American*, (New York: The Free Press, 1999), 208-213.

anniversary of Independence Day drew closer, both men had received many requests for speeches and words to be shared at the various celebrations. Thomas Jefferson was too ill at that point to attend the celebrations, but did write a statement:

> May it be to the world, what I believe it will be, (to some parts sooner, to others later, but finally to all,) the signal of arousing men to burst the chains under which monkish ignorance and superstition had persuaded them to bind themselves, and to assume the blessings and security of self-government. ...These are grounds of hope for others; for ourselves, let the annual return of this day forever refresh our recollections of these rights, and an undiminished devotion to them.[46]

Thomas Jefferson went into a coma on July 3, 1826, and lived until noontime on the Fourth of July. John Adams collapsed in his reading chair on the morning of the Fourth and lingered until late in the afternoon. The two friends and Founding Fathers left their cause in this world to the hands of the next generations.

July 1955; November 1956; March 1973

Three dates of tragedies for one person to endure have made one woman stronger. A young mother of two was struck by breast cancer. Georgia Goranites Bouchles lost her battle with cancer and left behind an eight-year-old daughter, Olympia, and a twelve-year-old son, John, and her husband in 1955. A year later in November 1956, George Bouchless, the father to the two children, died of heart disease. The first two tragedies occurred within sixteen months of each other. The third in 1973

---

[46] Joseph J. Ellis, *Founding Brothers; The Revolutionary Generation,* (New York: Random House, 2000), 246.

robbed a young wife of her husband when he was killed in a car accident. These three dates are moments that Senator Olympia Snowe of Maine has embedded in her memory. With each loss, one person endured the future. She could have been a victim of the loss of both parents at such a young age and the loss of a young husband, but Olympia has overcome the hardships that most people never face with the goal of public service and helping others.

Reminiscing about the sudden death of her husband, Peter, Olympia said:

> With the devastation of Peter's death came a sensitivity to the tremendous difficulties that other women in similar situations can face—such as raising children alone. Later that was brought to bear on issues such as pension reform, child care, and displaced homemakers.[47]

Three significant dates that Olympia Snowe will never forget, even though she has moved forward from the grief and faced each new day.

October 26, 1984

Paul Brosious worked at IBM and lived in Shrub Oak, New York, with his wife and four children. He had been in good health and had shown no signs of illness. He was at work on October 25, 1984, when he started experiencing searing pains through his chest. His coworkers thought he was having a heart attack, but the diagnosis came back as an aortic aneurysm. It is described as a small hole in the aorta, which prevents enough blood to get to the heart. He was a very sick man and died before the hospital had been able to move him to another facility to operate.

---

[47] Catherine Whitney, *Nine and Counting: The Women of the Senate*, (New York: HarperCollins, 2000), 70.

Lisa Beamer's father had played an influential role in the shaping of his daughter. His sudden illness and consequential death caused great grief for the family. Lisa faced many questioning moments, and feelings of total loss at the unexpected death of her father, yet God's peace was eventually revealed to her and perhaps that is what gave her strength once again when her life was radically changed on another tragic date.[48]

September 7, 2001

Days after a successful eleven-hour surgery, Matt Cole was on the road to recovery—again. He had endured a traumatic fourteen months of surgeries, chemotherapy treatments, radiation and recovery from the deadly juvenile cancer, Ewing Sarcoma. It is a rare bone cancer usually found in children under the age of 18; however, Matt was 19 years old, in the Army and in bad shape when he was diagnosed. He had been having health problems, but never received a clear diagnosis, when finally, the doctors realized what they were dealing with and were giving him a grim prognosis. The young fighter went on to prove the doctors wrong and in the spring of 2001 had beaten the deadly disease and was considered a cancer survivor.

The strong former high-school football star and all-around American guy could no longer fulfill his dream of being a soldier so he enrolled in college, had a job and a girlfriend when things took a turn for the worse. Matt's body was rejecting a prosthetic rib cage that had replaced his disease-ridden rib cage. In early September 2001, he underwent surgery to correct the problem. The doctors were relieved to find that the cancer had not returned and were optimistic that Matt would recover.

---

[48] Lisa Beamer, *Let's Roll*, (Wheaton, IL: Tyndale House, Inc., 2002), 62.

A couple of days later, as he was visiting with his stepmother, Sherrie, he rolled over in pain. A blood clot had traveled through his body and instantly took his life. He left behind a grieving family, several hundred friends and a life full of promise. My cousin, Matt, was taken from this life one month before his 21st birthday.

Dates are very important. Time is what we measure our days and lives by, and how we use time, can determine who we become. Although we may question why, there are no specific answers to why anyone on any day. Why was my life spared when thousands of other women's lives have been taken by breast cancer? In battle, why is one soldier saved and the other lost. There is not always an answer to our questions of why, but there is always the assurance that someone far bigger than human beings has the puzzle completed, while we are still looking for the pieces to fit.

Chapter 10
Other Dates of Significance

Not a day passes over this earth but men and women of note
do great deeds, speak great words and suffer noble sorrows.
                                                        –Charles Reed

IF WE TOOK EVERY DATE on the calendar, there would probably be long lists of noteworthy events for all 365 days of the year. The reason is because there are so many important events that have formed the earth since the beginning of time. There is no way we can recognize every significant historical date, but by using a few dates, we point out how every day is important and each day starts with a clean slate before us. We may have some control over how the day turns out, but many times, life-shattering events happen that we had never planned for. Then there are those dates that were planned and made headlines from what took place.

May 21, 1881

Clara Barton dominated the early history of the American Red Cross, which was modeled after the International Red Cross. She did not originate the Red Cross idea, but she was the first person to establish a lasting Red Cross Society in America. She successfully organized the American Association of the Red Cross in Washington, D.C., created to serve America in peace and in war, during times of disaster and national calamity. Barton's organization took its service beyond that of the International Red Cross Movement by adding disaster relief to battlefield assistance. She served as the organization's volunteer president until 1904.[49]

May 21, 1927

The *Spirit of St. Louis* flown by Charles Lindbergh made its first flight from New York to Paris across the Atlantic. It took 33 hours for the successful flight and was the beginning of millions of flights.[50] Where would our society be today without the availability of airplane travel? That day not only changed the way we travel, but our world has become more global because of the use of airplanes. The risks taken by Charles Lindburgh and others like him changed the way we do business, the landscape of relocated families, tourism, and war.

January 22, 1973

Roe v. Wade was passed by the Supreme Court and legalized abortion. That day many millions of lives were lost. Abortion became easily accessible and an alternate form of birth control was implemented for the carelessness of young men and women. The cries from the graves will forever ring in our ears as we allow the lives of unborn babies to be discarded for the sake of family planning. One date changed the course of millions of lives and may have snuffed out the person who would find the cure to cancer. It may have destroyed the person who would have brought peace to the Middle East. That day

---

[49]Candice Ransom, *Clara Barton,* (Minneapolis: Lerner Publications Company, 2003), 36.

[50] Arthur M. Schlesinger, Jr., *The Almanac of American History*, (New York: Barnes & Noble Books, Inc., 1993), 449.

may have left behind a beautiful choir of voices that would have soothed hurting Americans. The argument can be made that many women would have lost their lives from illegal abortions or women would have found alternative ways to eliminate the heart that beat within her, but had it not been legal, it would have been illegal, therefore fewer abortions would have been performed and fewer lives would have been taken. That was a significant date indeed.

September 25, 1981

Sandra Day O'Connor took the oath of office and was sworn in to the United States Supreme Court as the first female justice. The Stanford University Law School graduate had come a long way from the Lazy B Ranch in Arizona to find a place on the U.S. Supreme Court at the appointment of President Ronald Reagan. Her frontier life in Arizona and Texas taught her much about a different type of frontier as she blazed a trail for women and a trail for herself as a Supreme Court Justice.[51]

To make things happen, steps have to be taken and choices have to be made. Then there is a date that stands out to show the accomplishment of those pathways taken toward progress. Every day should be a continuation of yesterday's choices and preparation for tomorrow's outcome.

---

[51] Sandra Day O'Connor and H. Alan Day, *Lazy B: Growing Up on a Cattle Ranch in the American Southwest,* (New York: Random House, 2002).

Summary of Part II

THROUGHOUT OUR LIVES WE EACH encounter more monotonous and less momentous parts of life, and each of those days are lived by breathing, eating, working and sleeping. At the close of the day we may fall into bed from sheer exhaustion, utter frustration, or complete satisfaction depending on what events take place to shape our world. When we encounter sleeplessness it can be attributed to stress related issues or something else, but our day has ended nevertheless and a new day lies on the horizon. For many, getting through each day is a task, but for others, getting through each day and looking forward to tomorrow is a blessing—something for which to be thankful. This is a choice. The decision to worry and fret about each second of life takes energy, but we can choose to be thankful for the life we live. No life is idyllic and nothing in life is perfect, but looking at the glass as half full lends optimism for the future. Sometimes life's simplest moments give us the largest lessons.

After getting over the initial shock of the breast cancer diagnosis, I was thankful to God for a fighting chance. The diagnosis came only a few months after September 11, 2001, and I was reminded that all the doctors, surgeons and medicine in the world could not help those who were on the planes or in the buildings that day. I thought of my cousin, Matt, whose life had been taken away one month before his twenty-first birthday. There is always someone in worse shape, and if you think you have it worse than anyone else, then perhaps you do or possibly it's all in the attitude.

The biggest part to living a whole and complete life is doing just that—living.

Part III
Historical Dates from the Life of Christ

It is the heart always that sees before the head can see.
–Thomas Carlyle

THIS NEXT PHASE OF THE book delves deep into history to find out how faith can and does play a role in each life. With a look at the life of Jesus Christ, we can find the answers to many questions, and questions for what we once had answers for—or so we thought.

Throughout generations and dynasties, there have been the men who have developed large followings according to their beliefs. Historical accounts document the paths of how four of the most recent and prominent men who have achieved dictatorial status gained their large followings, which allowed them to become notorious dictators. Saddam Hussein, Adolf Hitler, Fidel Castro and Osama Bin Laden have caused total devastation, and hurt to millions of people and have been the cause of several wars and cultural crises. Throughout history comparisons have been made between other dictators, religious zealots and Jesus; however, the difference between hatred and love is evidenced in the life of only one.

Jesus was being hailed as a blasphemer and some sort of cult leader or dictatorial leader, which is why the leadership of that time period had to do away with Him. The decision makers and haters of Jesus did not take into account His virgin birth, sinless nature, His ability to perform miracles and His

81

recognition to be God. Even still, the world was changed on the day He was born, the day He died and the day He rose from the dead.

But how is the life of Jesus Christ important in a book about significant dates? That question is about to be answered in the following chapters as we contemplate how one day can change one life by one decision.

Chapter 11
December 25, 5 B.C.–The Birth of Christ

I am the voice of one calling in the desert, 'Make straight the way for the Lord.'

–John the Baptist

Christmas Day

Although most theologians agree that December 25 was not likely the actual birth date of the baby Jesus, the date is one in which Christians around the world celebrate the holy arrival of their savior. The event in 5 or 6 B.C. was uneventful to those who were looking for a royal birth because it took place in a dirty stable filled with animals in the small town of Bethlehem. A gentile doctor named Luke recorded the story. Luke's account of the birth of Jesus of Nazareth is detailed to some extent, but his actual declaration of the birth is one short sentence that reads, "*While they were there,* [Bethlehem] *the time came for the baby to be born, and she gave birth to her firstborn, a son.*" Luke 2:6-7 (NIV)

The grandness of the arrival was missing. There was no palace or kingly welcome, only a barn and an animal feeding trough to welcome this remarkable baby. What's more amazing about His birth is that Biblical accounts declare that the birth of Christ fulfilled the prophecies of the Old Testament prophets who talked about the coming Messiah as the savior of the world hundreds of years before His arrival.

The importance of that date changed the calendar. This one person changed the world from the moment He entered the scene.

The story of the nativity is well known, but there are unanswered logistical questions, like:

Why was there no room in the inn? Could it possibly be symbolic to the hearts of people since we are so filled with ourselves that we have little room left for the One who can free us from ourselves?

Another question worth asking is why was God's timing for Mary's delivery while a census was being taken, which then required Mary to travel during her final days of pregnancy? Maybe the trip was a way of God reminding us of the difficulties we all must overcome in our journey through life and by having God as our guide; we will not lose our way.

Why were no other people on hand to witness the birth? Perhaps, God's hope for people would be that we would not complicate the most sacred birth. Or, perhaps God was looking for believers based on simple faith.

Christ's birth is one of the most important and celebrated historical dates, so let's take a walk back and listen to those who were there watching and participating during one of the biggest events of all time.

Mary, the Mother of Jesus

A young teenager was chosen to be the mother of Jesus, and before Mary's encounter with the Angel Gabriel she was not mentioned. Recently engaged to a young carpenter named Joseph, Mary knew in her heart that it was not possible for her to be pregnant because they had not slept together. However, when Gabriel made his pronouncement to Mary, his words were carefully and divinely executed, "*Greetings, you who are highly favored! The Lord is with you."* (Luke 1:28)

Imagine seeing another being, someone who is not human, and hear him say those words to you? Do you think Mary was thinking of all the negative things about herself and focusing on her faults and that this Angel must have made a mistake? Mary may have looked around the room to make sure that Gabriel was talking to her and not somebody else.

Luke goes on to describe the scene: *"Mary was greatly troubled at his words and wondered what kind of greeting this might be."* (v. 29)

"Troubled" is a nice way to say "scared out of her wits!" Visualize this scene. Mary is very young—much younger than the average woman is today when she is getting married. She didn't have years of boyfriends, baggage and experience to prepare her for something so big. However, she was obviously favored in the sight of God, which says a lot about her character.

> *"Do not be afraid, Mary, you have found favor with God. You will be with child and give birth to a son, and you are to give him the name Jesus. He will be great and will be called the Son of the Most High. The Lord God will give him the throne of his father David, and he will reign over the house of Jacob forever; his kingdom will never end."*
>
> *"How will this be," Mary asked the angel, "since I am a virgin?"*
>
> *The angel answered, "The Holy Spirit will come upon you, and the power of the Most High will overshadow you. So the holy one to be born will be called the Son of God. Even Elizabeth your relative is going to have a child in her old age, and she who was said to be barren is in her sixth month. For nothing is impossible with God."*
>
> (Luke 1:30-37)

Wow! Gabriel did not mince any words with his proclamation. He told her the facts and what she needed to do and the rest was up to the Holy Spirit and God. After learning all of this, Mary's response was, "*I am the Lord's servant... May it be to me as you have said.*"

She sees and hears nothing but this out-of-body being proclaiming that she:

1. Has "found favor with God."
2. Will be "with child."
3. Will have a son.
4. Will name him Jesus.
5. He will be great and will be called the Son of the Most High.
6. He will be given the throne of his great (x 25) grandfather, David.
7. He will reign over the house of Jacob (the nation of Israel) forever.
8. His kingdom will never end.

Mary's mind must have been working a mile a minute as she tried to comprehend all that was being said. Did she wonder what type of experience it would be to have the power of the Most High overshadow her? What does that mean? These are questions that Mary may have thought of, but Mary's faith is the reason why she was chosen to be the mother of Jesus. Her simple faith brought her to the stable in Bethlehem to be a participant in the greatest birth ever known to mankind.

Joseph, the Earthly Father of Jesus

It had been a long road to Bethlehem for Joseph. The only reason he and Mary had traveled so far from their home in Nazareth was because Caesar Augustus demanded that a census of the entire Roman world be taken; therefore, Joseph had to register in his hometown. Mary was very pregnant at this time, but there was no way out for Joseph. He had to participate in the census. The last nine months could not have been an easy time for him, due to the circumstances. He had found out that the woman he was planning to marry was pregnant, and he knew it could not be his child because he had not slept with her. The obvious choice would be to break off the relationship and move on, but that's not what Joseph did. Not because he was not disturbed and mistrustful of Mary, but because of a dream.

> *Joseph, son of David, do not be afraid to take Mary home as your wife, because what is conceived in her is from the Holy Spirit. She will give birth to a son, and you are to give him the name Jesus, because he will save his people from their sins.* (Matt. 1:20-21)

Now, imagine this was you. You woke up from this weird dream where an angel told you that your fiancée was pregnant with the Holy Spirit's child. Would there be some questions? Would you be a little confused?

> *When Joseph woke up, he did what the angel of the Lord had commanded him and took Mary home as his wife. But he had no union with her until she gave birth to a son. And he gave him the name, Jesus.* (Matt. 1:24)

This is another example of simple faith by a simple man. God chose Joseph because he knew the breadth of his faith, the strength of his character and the depth of his love for Mary.

Why did Joseph and Mary arrive in Bethlehem so late that they were not able to find a room in one of the Inns? Obviously without modern conveniences and telephones there was no way to dial 1-800-HOTEL and make a reservation, but was there no opportunity for Joseph to write to a relative or friend to have something ready for he and Mary? Since Bethlehem was the town of Joseph's birth, would he not have had relatives living in Bethlehem that would have allowed them to stay? These questions are not answered in any of the gospel accounts of the birth of Christ; however, the answer could be as simple as God's desire for his son's birth to be uncomplicated by humans.

The pictures and Christmas pageants portray a quiet stable with animals and no other people but Mary and Joseph to witness this special and miraculous birth. What was it like to be there? Only Mary and Joseph know and neither of them wrote about it.

The Shepherds

The shepherds were hanging out in the field counting sheep when they first encountered the Star. They may have been talking about their girlfriends and other troubles of the day or playing their musical instruments. They had no idea what was taking place not far from them in a stable.

"An angel of the Lord appeared to them, and the glory of the Lord shone around them, and they were terrified." (Luke 2:9)

Terrified is an excellent term for what must have been earth shattering to the shepherds. Many times shepherds were young, teenage boys—not even men yet, so their terror would be magnified by the sheer chance that they were young and helpless in a field with sheep.

"Do not be afraid, I bring you good news of great joy that will be for all the people. Today in the town of David a Savior has been born to you; he is Christ the Lord." (Luke 2:10-11)

The angel saw their terror and addressed it right away. From the way Luke describes the scene, it sounds like the angel is happy and excited, but is sure to calm the fears of the shepherds. The whole panorama is a magnificent and exciting one that is replayed every Christmas; however, the scene that we play at Christmastime is just the beginning of the life Christ would lead over the next 33 years.

We often see three shepherds, but Luke did not state the number of shepherds or their ages. We know that the first people to have contact with Jesus outside of Joseph and Mary were these simple, humble shepherds. Why is that? Why wasn't the announcement of the Messiah made to the nobles and greats? Could it have been because they would not have believed that a Messiah would come from such unsophisticated, uneducated people? After all, Mary and Joseph were not blue blooded. Maybe the shepherds were told because God knew they would have faith and believe. Not only did the shepherds leave their flocks to go visit the new baby, but they left the stable and told everyone they could that the Messiah had arrived.

> *When they had seen him, they spread the word concerning what had been told them about this child, and all who heard it were amazed at what the shepherds said to them.* (Luke 2:17-18)

So the shepherds left the sheep (I wonder what happened to those sheep) and told everyone they could about this special birth. Do you suppose they would have been laughed at? I'm sure there were many that would not listen to one word a shepherd would say, but the shepherds were the ones chosen to be Christ's first visitors and messengers. They were there on the one most historic day in history.

Every year Christmas is a huge celebration both commercially and religiously. But just because a traditional religion is followed, does not mean that we have all the answers to all of the questions. Perhaps not knowing all of the facts relating to Christ's birth is God's way of asking us to trust. It's easy to believe when all the answers are available to us; then faith would never be required. There will always be unanswered questions about the birth of Christ, because not all of the facts are written about in the Gospels or the rest of the Bible. We can speculate about the logistics of the stable and why there were no other family members or friends involved in the prominent birth celebration, but the reality remains that according to Biblical accounts, the day of Christ's birth impacted our world as we know it. Christmas in 5 B.C. was monumental. That day changed history and it still impacts the future as Christmas continues to be a time of anticipation, celebration and worship.

Chapter 12
April 7, A.D. 30—Good Friday

*Forgiveness is the remission of sins. For it is by this that what
has been lost, and was found, is saved from being lost again.*
                                                        −Saint Augustine

Good Friday

The day of Christ's death was a day of doom for the
followers of Jesus Christ, but even more so for Jesus who was
betrayed by one of his own disciples. Have you ever felt
betrayed by someone close to you? Most of us have, but we
could never relate to how Jesus must have felt when He knew
that He had to take the sins of the world to a horrible death.
When Judas arrived with the guards and handed Jesus over to
them, the utter betrayal of all society was in that one act of
hatred. Biblical accounts of Christ's death portray the humanity
of Jesus as he was beaten and dragged through the streets with
blood dripping off his body marking the path to the cross. Each
drop of blood was for a world gone amuck by the sins of Adam
and Eve and the whole human race.

Christ's death was to allow the world a new avenue directly
to God…the avenue was belief in Christ as the Son of God, the
Savior of the World and Redeemer of the sinful nature of
humanity. Good Friday is a solemn day even two thousand
years later, but not nearly as solemn as the date that changed
the world.

Now the Feast of Unleavened Bread, called the Passover,
was approaching, and the chief priests and the teachers of
the law were looking for some way to get rid of Jesus, for
they were afraid of the people. (Luke 22:1-2)

April 7, A.D. 30

The political plot was about to climax as the Passover approached that year. The Jewish leaders were becoming more skeptical of Jesus and were looking for ways to eliminate him. Their fierce determination to find Jesus guilty of blasphemy—since he claimed to be God—was at the forefront of their need to destroy Him. The leaders did not want the people affected by the teachings of Jesus Christ. He taught in the Temple regularly and wherever he went people followed to listen to Him.

Questions of a sudden famed leader were rightly raised because, as we know from past experience, dictators rise and have a great following only to be destructive to those they are leading. However, the difference was Jesus' way of leading. He did not lead by stifling others or hurting people. He led by:

- calling the humble
- healing the sick
- feeding the hungry
- restoring sight to the blind
- helping the lost find their way

Jesus' leadership was by serving and meeting the needs of others. Notice all the words to describe his style were verbs—meaning action. He was not looking to be worshipped or to be served. His whole purpose was to point the world to God. Good Friday was the end to God as a man, but just the beginning for salvation from the sin of man through faith and belief in Jesus Christ.

Pontius Pilate

Pilate was the Roman official in charge of the administrative district; therefore the governor of the province of Judea, where Jerusalem was located. Early on this morning, an angry crowd from the Sanhedrin dragged a bound Jesus and placed Him before Pilate. The Sanhedrin had quietly met during the middle night hours to quicken the guilty verdict for Jesus. Pilate was not a strong man of character who stood on principle, rather he struggled politically and was susceptible to folding in pressure situations, which is exactly what Caiphas and other ruling members were hoping for that early morning. They needed to have Jesus crucified immediately because it was the custom that a prisoner chosen by the crowd be released during the feast. There was a notorious criminal named Barabbas who should have been crucified, but the crowd, led by Caiphas, wanted him to be released and Jesus to be crucified in his place. The guilty verdict and crucifixion had to take place rapidly due to the approaching Sabbath.

> *"Are you the king of the Jews?" asked Pilate.*
> *"Yes, it is as you say," Jesus replied.*
> *The chief priests accused him of many things. So again Pilate asked him, "Aren't you going to answer? See how many things they are accusing you of."* (Mark 15:2-5)

Pilate knew in his heart that Jesus had done nothing wrong, but as the acting official he had to follow through with his job of questioning. Not only did he not want to hand down a guilty verdict to an innocent man, but he had to return to his wife who had told him to have nothing to do with Jesus.

> *While Pilate was sitting on the judge's seat, his wife sent him this message: "Don't have anything to do with that innocent man, for I have suffered a great deal today in a dream because of him."* (Matt. 27:19)

Pilate considered his wife's warning, but he was more concerned about his political career and a possible riot from the crowd if he did not act to crucify Jesus.

> *"Do you want me to release to you the king of the Jews?"*
> *asked Pilate, knowing it was out of envy that the chief*
> *priests had handed Jesus over to him. But the chief priests*
> *stirred up the crowd to have Pilate release Barabbas*
> *instead.*
> *"What shall I do, then, with the one you call the king of*
> *the Jews?" Pilate asked them.*
> *"Crucify him!" they shouted.*
> *"Why? What crime has he committed?" asked Pilate.*
> *But they shouted all the louder, "Crucify him!"*
> *Wanting to satisfy the crowd, Pilate released Barabbas*
> *to them. He had Jesus flogged, and handed him over to be*
> *crucified."* (Mark 15:9-15)

Pilate literally washed his hands to be free from his own guilt of handing over an innocent man to death. The guilty man who should have been put to death was Barabbas; however, he was set free. Pilate did not stand firm on his belief that Jesus truly was not guilty of any wrongdoing. He followed the crowd's cries and stooped from facing any criticism by the other rulers. His decision was a crucial one and was a part of what Jesus said was God's plan.

Judas Iscariot

The day of Christ's death all started with the act of Judas, the one who betrayed Jesus and handed Him over to the religious leaders and Roman soldiers to be killed. Judas was selfish and greedy.

Then Satan entered Judas, called Iscariot, one of the Twelve. And Judas went to the chief priests and the officers of the temple guard and discussed with them how he might betray Jesus. They were delighted and agreed to give him money. He consented, and watched for an opportunity to hand Jesus over to them when no crowd was present. (Luke 22:3-6)

Judas actually never even made it to Christ's death because he hanged himself out of guilt before the crucifixion took place.

When Judas, who had betrayed him, saw that Jesus was condemned, he was seized with remorse and returned the thirty silver coins to the chief priests and the elders. "I have sinned," he said, "for I have betrayed innocent blood."

"What is that to us?" they replied. "That's your responsibility." So Judas threw the money into the temple and left. Then he went away and hanged himself. (Matt. 27:3-5)

This suicidal act of Judas raises the question of why he handed Jesus over to begin with if he knew that Jesus was who He claimed to be. It all started when Judas went to the chief priests looking for a ransom payment if he handed Jesus over to them. He received 30 pieces of silver for his act of betrayal. His decision to hand Jesus over had been made even before he asked for a ransom; it had been made by evil intent in his heart. Judas Iscariot played a crucial role in what became Good Friday in A.D. 30. His betrayal could be looked upon as the greatest mistake in history.

Simon from Cyrene

Talk about being in the wrong place at the wrong time! This guy just happens to be passing by; probably checking out what all of the ruckus was about when he was abruptly pulled aside and a cross was shoved on his shoulders as he was pushed ahead of Jesus. He had to carry the cross.

"As they led him [Jesus] *away, they seized Simon from Cyrene, who was on his way in from the country, and put the cross on him and made him carry it behind Jesus."* (Luke 23:26)

What must that have been like? Did he know whose cross he was carrying? Did he understand the job that had been forced upon him as he dragged the rough, heavy, burdensome cross to hold the proclaimed Savior of the world? Not much is known about this man, but he played a key position in the date that revamped history.

Good Friday ended with a distraught and torn apart community. Immediately prior to the execution of Christ, there were guards and soldiers who adamantly followed the crowd of accusers, but then changed their minds as Jesus' death was secured. The record in the Gospels says that some of them were convinced that Jesus was who he claimed to be upon his death. What changed their minds?

> *With a loud cry, Jesus breathed his last. The curtain of the temple was torn in two from top to bottom. And when the centurion, who stood there in front of Jesus, heard his cry and saw how he died, he said, "Surely this man was the Son of God!"* (Mark 15:37-39)

With the death of Christ the whole world changed. There were those who became believers of Jesus Christ and his message of redemption and salvation and there were those who turned their backs and continued in their traditional beliefs and political venues. One date changed how we look at God, Heaven, Hell, religion and life.

In Og Mandino's book, *The Christ Commission*, he describes the type of life Jesus led and what He left behind at His death:

> He left behind no gold, no silver, no land, no wife, no children, no manuscripts, no works of art, and no position of authority or title. Furthermore, he was not even among us for very long. Most great men whose words or actions have changed the course of our world have required six or seven decades or more in order to accomplish their purpose. And even their deeds, so great at the time, soon fade from our memory. This man died while still in his thirties, and yet nothing he has done or said has ever diminished even a little.[52]

---

[52] Og Mandino, *The Christ Commission*, (New York: Bantam Books, 1980), 236.

Chapter 13
April 9, A.D. 30—Resurrection Day

Sorrow looks back, worry looks around, faith looks up.
                                                    —Guideposts

Easter

Various denominations in the Christian community refer to Easter as 'Resurrection Day' because it was the day that the Bible ascertains Jesus rose from the dead. The Bible tells how the stone to the tomb where Jesus' body had been laid was rolled away and Jesus appeared in a new body to those whom he loved and his disciples—the twelve who followed him.

Those who had insisted that Jesus was guilty of blaspheming God were afraid that some of the followers of Jesus would steal his body from the tomb. However, others remembered Jesus' words:

> *"Sir," they said, "we remember that while he was still alive that deceiver said, 'After three days I will rise again.' So give the order for the tomb to be made secure until the third day. Otherwise, his disciples may come and steal the body and tell the people that he has been raised from the dead."*
>
> *"Take a guard," Pilate answered. "Go, make the tomb as secure as you know how." So they went and made the tomb secure by putting a seal on the stone and posting the guard.* (Matthew 27:63-66)

On the third day, the stone to the tomb had been pushed aside; the seal had been broken and the body of Jesus was gone, but the linen cloths that they had wrapped the body in were still there. It was the first day of the week, which is now the day Christians recognize as "The Lord's Day."

Why all the hype for Easter? We know that Easter is the date that Christianity celebrates the resurrection of the Savior. The implication of the resurrection is that Christ came to take the sins of the world upon his shoulders—that was his death. Because he took the sins of the world to the cross, he could now return to heaven with God and reign as God. He was no longer a man.

Easter has become a holiday that symbolizes the coming of flowers and warmer weather, but the main significance of Easter is to celebrate this amazing resurrection. Believers and followers of Jesus note Easter as a holy time as they commune over what the resurrection meant. Their belief is that the Savior came back to life after being crucified, and with his resurrection new life is promised to all who believe and receive Him. However, being raised from the dead is not a common occurrence, and thus raises questions of how this could happen when there were numerous eyewitnesses to account for the death of Christ while his body and tomb were carefully guarded.

Mary Magdalene

This incredible woman has left a respectable legacy in Biblical history. First, she was a demon-possessed woman who was filled with wickedness and evil until Jesus rescued her and freed her from the demons.

"When Jesus rose early on the first day of the week, he appeared first to Mary Magdalene, out of whom he had driven seven demons." (Mark 16:9)

Once freed from demon-possession there was no turning

back for Mary Magdalene; she followed Jesus and was one of His few supporters who stood at the foot of the cross and witnessed his death. While Jesus' disciples, with the exception of John, were not present at the crucifixion, Mary Magdalene bravely stood as a witness of his death. She was also the first person to see him in his resurrected form.

Early on the first day of the week, while it was still dark, Mary Magdalene went to the tomb and saw that the stone had been removed from the entrance. So she came running to Simon Peter and the other disciple, the one Jesus loved, [John] and said, "They have taken the Lord out of the tomb, and we don't know where they have put him!"

So Peter and the other disciple started for the tomb. Both were running, but the other disciple outran Peter and reached the tomb first. He bent over and looked in at the strips of linen lying there but did not go in. Then Simon Peter, who was behind him, arrived and went into the tomb. He saw the strips of linen lying there, as well as the burial cloth that had been around Jesus' head. The cloth was folded up by itself, separate from the linen. Finally the other disciple, who had reached the tomb first, also went inside. He saw and believed...

Then the disciples went back to their homes, but Mary stood outside the tomb crying. As she wept, she bent over to look into the tomb and saw two angels in white, seated where Jesus' body had been, one at the head and the other at the foot.

They asked her, "Woman, why are you crying?"

"They have taken my Lord away," she said, "and I don't know where they have put him." At this, she turned around and saw Jesus standing there, but she did not realize that it was Jesus.

"Woman," he said, "why are you crying? Who is it you are looking for?"

Thinking he was the gardener, she said, "Sir, if you have carried him away, tell me where you have put him, and I will get him."

*Jesus said to her, "**Mary**." (John 20:1-16)*

It was at the point of her name being spoken that Mary Magdalene realized Jesus was alive and the one with whom she was speaking. His body had changed, but his voice must have been the same when he spoke her name. Think about the way your mother, father or spouse says your name when they want to get your attention. You know the sound and tone of that voice.

Mary Magdalene was very upset by the death of Jesus and even more so at the thought that His body had been stolen. Like the disciples, Mary had not understood Jesus' predictions of a bodily resurrection, but upon hearing His voice, she believed and went to tell the others how she had seen the risen Christ.

> *Jesus said, "Do not hold on to me, for I have not yet returned to the Father. Go instead to my brothers and tell them, I am returning to my Father and your Father, to my God and your God."*
>
> *Mary Magdalene went to the disciples with the news: "I have seen the Lord!" And she told them that he had said these things to her.* (John 20:17-18)

Two Disciples

There were two believers that were walking away from Jerusalem on the day of the Resurrection. Only one of the two disciples is named by Luke's account of what took place on the road to Emmaus.

> *Now that same day two of them were going to a village called Emmaus, about seven miles from Jerusalem. They were talking with each other about everything that had happened. As they talked and discussed these things with each other, Jesus himself came up and walked along with them; but they were kept from recognizing him.*
>
> *He asked them, "What are you discussing together as you walk along?"*

They stood still, their faces downcast. One of them, named Cleopas, asked him, "Are you only a visitor to Jerusalem and do not know the things that have happened there in these days?"

"What things?" he asked.

"About Jesus of Nazareth," they replied. "He was a prophet, powerful in word and deed before God and all the people. The chief priests and our rulers handed him over to be sentenced to death, and they crucified him; but we had hoped that he was the one who was going to redeem Israel. And what is more, it is the third day since all this took place. In addition, some of our women amazed us. They went to the tomb early this morning but didn't find his body. They came and told us that they had seen a vision of angels, who said he was alive. Then some of our companions went to the tomb and found it just as the women had said, but him they did not see."

He said to them, "How foolish you are, and how slow of heart to believe all that the prophets have spoken! Did not the Christ have to suffer these things and then enter his glory?" And beginning with Moses and all the Prophets, he explained to them what was said in all the Scriptures concerning himself.

As they approached the village to which they were going, Jesus acted as if he were going farther. But they urged him strongly, "Stay with us, for it is nearly evening; the day is almost over." So he went in to stay with them.

When he was at the table with them, he took bread, gave thanks, broke it and began to give it to them. Then their eyes were opened and they recognized him, and he disappeared from their sight. (Luke 24:13-31)

This whole series of conversations and events can be associated with the way people come to believe that Jesus was, in fact, God. Here were two disciples walking along talking about the events that happened with someone they thought was a complete stranger. Before the death of Christ they had believed Him to be God, but then as they are talking to Jesus they say that Jesus was a prophet. Fear kept them from revealing what they had believed. Their eyes were blinded by misunderstanding and unbelief. It was only after Jesus offered a prayer that they realized who the stranger was. Their unbelief stood in the way of knowing the resurrected Jesus.

Thomas

This man became known as "Doubting Thomas" because he did not believe the other disciples when they told him about Jesus' resurrection. Yet, for as much as he was labeled a "doubter," Thomas was also a very loyal follower of Christ and firm believer.

> *Now Tomas (called Didymus), one of the Twelve, was not with the disciples when Jesus came. So the other disciples told him, "We have seen the Lord!"*
> *But he said to them, "Unless I see the nail marks in his hands and put my finger where the nails were, and put my hand into his side, I will not believe it."* (John 20:24-25)

So, there you have it. His one statement labeled him for life. His statement probably sums up all of civilization because we cannot believe everything we hear or everything someone tells us. So questioning or doubting are positive traits; however, this particular case was different. We don't know that the disciples didn't play tricks on each other during their camaraderie as followers of Jesus. Perhaps Thomas had been picked on in the past, and like the others, he had not fully understood Jesus' words when He told them that He would be crucified and rise again on the third day. The story of the Last Supper shows that the disciples did not fully understand what Jesus was saying. Thomas did come around, though.

A week later his disciples were in the house again, and Thomas was with them. Though the doors were locked, Jesus came and stood among them and said, "Peace be with you!" Then he said to Thomas, "Put your finger here; see my hands. Reach out your hand and put it into my side. Stop doubting and believe."

Thomas said to him, "My Lord and my God!" (John 20:26-28)

Jesus knew that Thomas had not believed what the others had told him, but at the same time the others had seen Jesus and Thomas had not. Jesus wasted no time on small talk, but got right to the point with Thomas.

This particular scripture mentions that the doors were locked—the disciples were afraid that the rulers would find them and arrest them for following Christ so they were trying to maintain a low profile. It does not say that Jesus came and rang the doorbell, but that "*Jesus came and stood…*"

Christ's appearance must have been startling to the disciples because he just appeared—like a ghost. It was after he had shown his scars from the crucifixion that they believed and knew it was Jesus who stood before them.

"*Then Jesus told him, 'Because you have seen me, you have believed; blessed are those who have not seen and yet have believed.'*" (John 20-29)

Although Thomas doubted what he had been told by his peers, he believed and followed. When the disciples recognized that the life of Jesus was being threatened before he was arrested and crucified, Thomas was the one, who stood up and said, "*Let us also go, that we may die with him.*" (John 11:16) Yes, Thomas doubted, but his consistency was evidenced as a loyal follower of Christ.

After appearing to his disciples and reprimanding them for their unbelief in His resurrection, Jesus gave them this final message:

> *He said to them, "Go into all the world and preach the good news to all creation. Whoever believes and is baptized will be saved, but whoever does not believe will be condemned."* (Mark 16:15-16)

Easter is a beautiful time of year to ponder new life, its fragility and the belief that this life on earth is not all there is. The promise of God for those who believe in the reality and totality of Jesus' resurrection is a perfect life far from an imperfect world. A life that is lived with God in a place He calls heaven.

Chapter 14
The Most Important Day

The will of God will not take you where the grace of God cannot keep you.
—Anonymous

WE ARE GIVEN ONE LIFE to live and we never know when that life is going to end. We can celebrate life's beginning, but its ending is uncertain. Not knowing if tomorrow is going to be a date that is life changing can be unsettling or exciting, but what's more fearsome is what happens to us when our time on earth is done. Jesus taught much from the example He left for all of us to follow. From the two greatest commandments: *"Love the Lord your God with all your heart and with all your soul and with all your mind."* and *"Love your neighbor as yourself."* (Matthew 22:38-39) Following those commands and receiving the gift of new life from faith in Jesus as the Lord and Savior promises a heavenly home to believers. All of this comes from God's grace and mercy because of Christ's birth, death and resurrection.

Our faith in what God says is what is required—it is not being good or through doing good. Who defines good? And, could we ever be good enough? When Christ is present in our life, we are free to be who God desired for us to be all along. Good works are great, but when they are accompanied with a changed heart they have meaning and substance.

Generations have followed Christ's example and have begun a new life through a changed heart. The date a person gives his or her life to Jesus Christ is the most significant date in a person's life because it determines their outlook on life by the way they live, their dedication to faith and most importantly their destiny. The Bible is the timeless historical book that provides an explanation for mankind's fallen nature and a way of salvation.

Salvation is "the saving of a person from sin or its consequences especially in the life after death."[53]

Only through a realization of the need for a savior is life made whole and complete. It's not self-discovery or self-renewal that changes man's brokenness; it's God's son, Jesus Christ, the One whose life has been closely documented, studied and worshipped for over 2000 years. It is up to individuals to make the decision to believe whether Jesus Christ is the Savior or not. On the date that the choice is made, a life is changed and it becomes yet another mark of *one day*. People who have committed to faith in Christ have documented a date more important than any other in their lives:

A.D. 35

The Apostle Paul, a.k.a. Saul, was originally a radical religious leader and Pharisee. He was proud to uphold the original "Law" by persecuting those who followed Jesus Christ. After one of the disciples of Jesus was stoned to death, Saul went on a rampage to cleanse the whole district of Israel of Christians. He was mean, ruthless and relentless in his pursuit to weed out what he viewed as a cult-type of infiltration. However, his charge was halted instantaneously when he was on his way to flush out Jesus-followers in Damascus. The story of his conversion sounds unbelievable:

---

[53] *The New Merriam-Webster Dictionary*, (Springfield, MA: Merriam Webster, 1989).

> *As he neared Damascus on his journey, suddenly a light*
> *from heaven flashed around him. He fell to the ground and*
> *heard a voice say to him, "Saul, Saul, why do you*
> *persecute me?"*
> *"Who are you, Lord?" Saul asked.*
> *"I am Jesus, whom you are persecuting," he replied.*
> *"Now get up and go into the city, and you will be told what*
> *you must do."* (Acts 9:3-6)

Saul did what the voice told him and he continued to the house of a disciple named Ananias. After questioning the Lord, Ananias was a bit leery to go to see Saul because he knew that Saul tortured Christians. The story continued:

> *But the Lord said to Ananias, "Go! This man is my chosen*
> *instrument to carry my name before the Gentiles and their*
> *kings and before the people of Israel. I will show him how*
> *much he must suffer for my name."* (Acts 9:15-16)

Because of his personal conversion, Paul went on to be one of the most significant figures—apart from Christ—to shape Christianity. Through his missionary journeys outside of the Jewish realms and the letters he wrote that became books in the New Testament, history was changed by one man's conversion and belief in Jesus Christ. Paul was the primary leader and first evangelist who brought Christianity to the rest of the world.

September 28, 1931

For three years a man struggled with his beliefs. He had abandoned his parents' view of Christianity as a child and became an atheist, but his resistance to his atheistic tendencies and search for the meaning of life changed one day while he and his brother were on their way to visit Whipsnade Zoo. C. S. Lewis found exactly what he had been looking for as he surrendered his life to Christ. He explains his conversion,

"When we set out I did not believe that Jesus Christ is the Son of God, and when we reached the zoo I did."[54]

C. S. Lewis became a renowned writer of many Christian and academic works. One of his most notable books is *The Lion, the Witch and the Wardrobe* from *The Chronicles of Narnia* series for children. God took his heart and made a beautiful, lasting masterpiece through the written words of C. S. Lewis.

November 1934

A young sixteen-year-old had been depending on church membership and his parents' faith to guarantee a relationship with God, yet one evening changed his outlook. Billy Graham realized that faith had to come from his own belief and that he had to make that decision. He realized that none of the rituals like reciting the Apostles' Creed or taking communion, or doing good could save him from the sin nature that he was born with.

Billy Graham remembers how his life took 'The 180-Degree Turn':

> What was slowly dawning on me during those weeks was the miserable realization that I did not know Jesus Christ for myself. I could not depend on my parents' faith. Christian influence in the home could have a lasting impact on a child's life, but faith could not be passed on as an inheritance, like the family silver. It had to be exercised by each individual. I could not depend on my church membership either.[55]

---

[54]Bruce L. Edwards, *The Chronicles of C.S. Lewis* Fact Sheet.
[55] Billy Graham, *Just As I Am,* (San Francisco: Harper Collins Worldwide; Zondervan, 1997), 28.

The verse that Billy Graham remembers as changing his direction was found in the book of Romans in the New Testament of the Bible. It states:

"But God commendeth his love toward us, in that, while we were yet sinners, Christ died for us." (Romans 5:8, KJV)

After putting his faith and trust in Jesus Christ, Billy Graham did not look back, but he plodded forward sharing with the world how a simple faith in Jesus Christ can transform anyone who believes.

July 1995

Over twenty years after abortion had been legalized in the United States of America by the Supreme Court's Roe v. Wade decision, Jane Roe, a.k.a. Norma McCorvey, made a decision that changed not only her life, but her view that the abortion movement had brought about since its legalization in 1973. Norma McCorvey had felt the pressure of a spiritual void in her life for many years, but she kept repressing those feelings until some caring and loving people took her under their wings and prayed for her. On a summer July night, Norma, a.k.a. Roe, realized her need of a savior and found that need met when she listened to the message that was spoken by Reverend Morris Sheats, Pastor of Hillcrest Church in Dallas, Texas. Several months of conscience searing accounts had brought Norma to the place of realizing that nothing she had done could not be erased and forgiven by a relationship with Jesus Christ. As she prayed and poured her heart out to the One who listens to every person, she felt her heart shift and mold into a pliable tool for Jesus Christ.

Prior to that date, Norma McCorvey told a reporter that, "This issue is the only thing I live for. I live, eat, breathe, think everything about abortion."[56]

Her views of Christians and pro-lifers were radically changed as she became acquainted with Christians and started making new friends within the Christian community.

> What startled me so much about the Christians at church and at Rescue [Operation Rescue] was how their attitudes were exactly the opposite of what I expected. In the abortion movement, we always assumed that Christians were mean-spirited, judgmental, pleasure-hating radicals. If they opened their mouths at all, we thought, it was only to condemn sinners and deliver a sermon about the wages of wickedness.
>
> In fact, I found out that *we* were the ones who were mean-spirited, self-righteous, and judgmental. It was those in the abortion movement who were ruled by hatred and spite. My entire frame of reference had changed.[57]

Since that date in 1995, her life has been turned upside down as she has pursued work in pro-life formats and has ended her long abortion advocacy. Her vision of life and the importance of every beating heart were changed on one significant day. But it wasn't just about abortion, it was about one life that was affected by the decision she made on one day.

March 8, 1997

A youth retreat involving a few hundred teenagers took place in Estes Park, Colorado. Cassie Bernall attended the retreat with a new friend she had made at Christian Fellowship School. Cassie's parents had insisted that she attend this private

---

[56] Norma McCorvey, *Won by Love*, (Nashville, TN: Thomas Nelson Publishers, 1997), 165.

[57] Ibid. 168.

school hoping that their daughter would find a different group of friends and refrain from the satanic lifestyle she had led with friends from her previous school. At this camp in the Rockies, Cassie was overwhelmed with the inspirational music and the theme of "overcoming the temptations of evil and breaking out of the selfish life." After the meeting, Cassie poured her heart out to God and found forgiveness and a transformed life that freed her from the chains of satanic worship. Cassie's life was changed from that day forward and she lived so that all who came in contact with her over the next two years would know that she believed in God and had faith.

Her mother, Misty Bernall, stated:

> For Cassie, March 8 not only meant the end of wallowing in anger and emptiness, confusion and despair, but the chance to begin a new chapter. Now life had a purpose beyond fighting back. Now there was hope.[58]

Cassie's faith may have been what cost her life on April 20, 1999, when she became a victim at Columbine High School. The story of her life and the U-turn that changed her has been a legacy that will live on in the lives of many teens that are living aimlessly and without purpose.

As children, we believe the rituals and traditions that our parents were taught when they were children and the religious cycle often continues unquestioned. Our religious beliefs are based on the traditions of the generations instead of our own need to know, and often we accept those beliefs taught by our parents and grandparents because it is all we know and all they knew to teach us. From Christ's teachings, the only way to have a relationship with God is individually; not on the coat

---

[58] Misty Bernall, *She Said Yes*, (New York: Pocket Books, 2000), 99.

tales of previous generations nor from previous traditions passed down.

Three dates of His 33 years on earth mark the most important decision of every person today: to believe or not to believe. It is our choice. In order to believe in God, there has to be some basis for the belief. Whether it is from our religious background, or from the comfort that a higher being has to offer. Belief in God is very different from having faith in God or trusting God. It is easy to believe, the harder part is having faith in what one cannot see and then living in faith of what One said.

Summary of Part III

JESUS CHRIST WAS A REAL person who has been followed through history. He cannot be dismissed as some sort of myth or nice religious guy when His very existence is documented from the beginning. Centuries have passed since His time on earth, but the legacy of His life is still followed today. The importance of His message and the evidence of the impact left behind continue to transform all who have encountered a deep personal and loving relationship with Him. His teachings and promises are easy enough for a child to understand and come to faith, but complex enough that even the smartest and best educated theological scholars are baffled by the mystery of His birth, His death and His resurrection. Uncomplicated faith is the difference. Some come to a saving knowledge of Jesus Christ by simply believing what He said and acknowledging their sin. Others reject Him after continuous study while they struggle with the meaning of life and death.

Your life can be changed like the lives touched by Christ when you admit the guilt of your sin and seek redemption from Christ. That's why He was born, why He died and why He rose again. It was all for you and me.

Part IV
One Day, One Life, One Decision

Some persons are very decisive when it comes to avoiding decisions.
–Brendan Francis

THIS BOOK HAS TAKEN THE past and linked it with the present. It has earmarked pertinent dates of famous people and noteworthy dates that made people famous; and it has brought us to the point of how and what we need to do about our own personal situation. None of the events or people we have studied can make decisions for us. It is up to each person. This fourth and final part of the book will be your own story of significant dates and events that have shaped your life and will bring you to the next level of moving forward and aspiring toward freedom from the past and preparation for the future.

Please remember as you read the following chapters and work on getting to know yourself that this part of the book stems from my own need to deal with myself. I would not ask you to do something I have not done myself. The next pages are not to throw a guilt trip your way, but to encourage you and motivate you to live life with no regrets and offer strategies to help you do that. If you are anything like me, many of these issues are things we, as humans, struggle with on a regular basis. I hope you are ready to step outside your comfort zone to find new perspective, refine your priorities and define your purpose.

This will be the hardest part of the book because work is

involved. From this point forward, you will be the one to do the work, but the outcome will be well worth it so that if tomorrow your life is changed, you will have prepared yourself in advance.

Chapter 15
The *One Day Method* for Life
Questions to Answer

*Nothing at all will be attempted if all possible objections
must first be overcome.*

–Samuel Johnson

AT THIS POINT YOU ARE probably thinking, "But what do
I do? I've read about all these people and dates that have
shaped history and life, but how can I change anything? What
should I do and how should I do it?"

Most of us have been in a situation of wondering what we
can do to change our lives or to get out of the rut we are in, so
if you are asking those questions or similar ones, start by taking
an inventory of what needs to be changed in your life and think
about a few things:

1) What would you still like to accomplish before
your life is over?
2) If you knew that tomorrow your life would
change, what would you do today to prepare for
that *one day*?
3) If you were told that you had one year to go back
and change the things you could to prepare for the
rest of your life, what changes would you make?

The Method

We have looked closely at the events that shape our ordinary lives and mold us into who we become. Our focus on the past may have left us with feelings of ineptitude and unimportance today. Those emotions may cause us to trudge through each day in survival mode unable to think about whether or not we are living life to the fullest. The *One Day Method* for making a difference in life pulls out all the stops and relies on you for the answers to your life and the reason you live the way you do. The strategy for living life by the philosophy of *One Day* needs necessary steps taken by you. You are the person that can make today important. Try the *One Day Method* and recognize some things about yourself that you may not have known or may not want to admit. By answering some tough questions about the real you, you may find the path toward living a life of significance. Now is the time for you to remove the mask you wear and find out what you believe in and who you really are.

ONE DAY METHOD: *Questions to ponder.*
Step One: Religious Background

- ♦ What are my religious beliefs?
- ♦ What is the basis for those beliefs? (What is the foundation? Bible, Church, a hierarchy, etc.)
- ♦ Why do I believe this foundation?
- ♦ How have these beliefs affected my life up until now?
- ♦ Do I believe that there is life after death and if so how do I attain that life?
- ♦ Do I believe I am guaranteed of this belief and what makes me sure?
- ♦ If I do not have a religious belief or am unhappy with my current belief, what can I do to change this?
- ♦ When will I start to change this?

Step Two: Childhood (Life at Home)

- What was my home life like as a child?
- Was I allowed choices growing up or was I told what to do and expected to do it without explanations?
- Were my parents a mostly positive influence in my life?
- What personality and parenting traits did I like best about my parents?
- What attitudes or behaviors did I most dislike about my parents?
- What were my happiest memories from childhood?
- What were the saddest parts of my childhood?
- Am I a victim of my childhood?
- Am I an overcomer of the things that happened in my childhood?
- In what ways did my childhood prepare me for the future?

Step Three: Adulthood

- How old was I when I left home?
- What was my reason for leaving home?
- What would I view as my three greatest achievements in life?
- Do I often blame others for my lack of achievements or what I view as failures?
- If I could change things about my past what would they be?
- Why would I change those things?
- What would I still like to accomplish in my life?
- What steps will I take to make those things happen?

Step Four: Marriage

♦   What attracted me to my mate?
♦   Before we were married what was my view of marriage and what were my expectations?
♦   Did I have second thoughts about marrying my mate?
♦   Would I say that our marriage is great, good, okay, bad or horrible?
♦   What makes our marriage great, good, okay, bad, or horrible?
♦   What can I do to improve the marriage?
♦   What could my mate do to improve the marriage?

Step Five: Parenting

♦   Am I a good parent?
♦   Why or why not?
♦   How do my children view me as a parent?
♦   Do I listen to my children?
♦   Do I spend too much time or not enough time with my children?
♦   Do my children see that they are a priority or are my priorities out of whack?
♦   What could I do to improve my parenting skills?

If you have reached this part of the book, stick with it, because you have just completed some of the biggest work. You have finally come to know yourself more intimately. You may now be admitting some things that were buried, and you may have realized a few things about yourself that you had either forgotten or never knew about.

All the questions listed in this chapter were questions that I had to answer when I was faced with cancer. I hadn't dared go too deep with myself to find out who I really was, but when I saw my life flashing before my eyes, I had to face those unanswered questions and deal with my life.

Being honest with ourselves about who we are is not easy, but once we have unveiled our hidden selves we can become true to who we are and who we want to become.

Chapter 16
The *One Day* Method for Life
Strategies for Improvement

Action springs not from thought, but from a readiness for responsibility.
—Dietrich Bonhoeffer

IN OUR EFFORTS TO AVOID conflict, most of us have developed this mechanism of zoning out. There is a wall that we are able to raise that makes us turn our back on the reality of a situation. Husbands use this state of zoning out to avoid dealing with a nagging wife; wives use it to avoid confronting an untrustworthy husband; children use it to avoid their parents and parents use it to ignore the reality that their kid is a monster and needs discipline! The most obvious use of the zone-out factor is how our culture uses it to ignore the need for God in our lives. If we don't think about our own mortality or our sin, then we deceive ourselves into thinking that we won't have to deal with those issues. The problem with the zone-out factor is that it never allows us to be totally honest with ourselves. When we do not face the facts that are right before us, we are choosing to lie and turn our backs on a situation that could be made better if we faced it head on. In essence, we use this mechanism to just get by in life without experiencing our full potential.

We are blessed, however, with overcoming life's disappointments if we reign in the zone-out factor and unleash what God has placed in each one of us—the ability to make choices. The first step to making changes in your life is to deal with those things you have zoned out for most of your life and use those efforts to move forward and fulfill the potential you have.

Now that you have answered some tough questions about yourself, review the following summarized strategies to implement changes that can encourage you to find a better way to live. Perhaps, like me, they will help you move in the right direction to make today the One Day that begins the rest of your life.

Step One: Religious Background

Nothing hath separated us from God but our own will,
or rather our own will is our separation from God.
— William Law

When you reflected on your religious background, what was the outcome? Are you confident in your belief and do you have an authority or foundation for what you believe? Are you certain of that authority? After reading about the events that shaped Jesus Christ's life, do you feel that He played a vital role in the shaping of the world, as we know it? If you are not secure in your beliefs, the best way to become secure is to begin searching for the truth. Start weeding through your knowledge or lack of knowledge by educating yourself.

Legal journalist and self-proclaimed atheist Lee Strobel did just that in his effort to discredit God. "To me, there was far too much evidence that God was merely a product of wishful thinking, of ancient mythology, of primitive superstition."[59]

Because of his beliefs, Strobel started his own investigation that resulted in his book, *The Case for Christ*, where he found more than what he was looking for.

---

[59] Lee Strobel, *The Case for Christ,* (Grand Rapids, MI: Zondervan Publishing House, 1998), 13.

On November 8, 1981, I realized that my biggest objection to Jesus also had been quieted by the evidence of history. I found myself chuckling at how the tables had been turned. In light of the convincing facts I had learned during my investigation, in the face of this overwhelming avalanche of evidence in the case for Christ, the great irony was this: it would require much more faith for me to maintain my atheism than to trust in Jesus of Nazareth!

After a personal investigation that spanned more than six hundred days and countless hours, my own verdict in the case for Christ was clear. However, as I sat at my desk, I realized that I needed more than an intellectual decision... Looking for a way to bring that about, I reached over to a Bible and opened it to John 1:12, a verse I had encountered during my investigation: "Yet to all who **received** him, to those who **believed** in his name, he **gave** the right to become children of God."[60]

For Lee Strobel and many others, their own investigation brought them to the timeless truths that are found from the life of Jesus Christ and the ancient manuscript of His life, the Bible. It is the key instrumental document that has continued to stand the test of time. If you have been struggling with your belief or unbelief in God, is it important enough to you to make the time to find out what God is all about? It's easier to accept hearsay or follow in comfortable traditions, but it's more fulfilling to learn and know why you believe what you believe. Reading the Bible on your own may give you some of the answers to the questions you have never asked. The New Testament is an excellent place to start your search since it deals directly with the Life of Jesus Christ.

Once you have discovered the truth of what you believe and find an authority for that basis, you will be amazed at how life may start falling into place. All your questions will never be

---

[60] Ibid., 259, 267.

answered, but the peace of knowing what you believe may aid you in discovering the real you. Today is the day to start nurturing your belief in God and His son, Jesus Christ.

Step Two: Childhood (Life at Home)

If you cannot get rid of the family skeleton, you may as well make it dance.
                                                                    –George Bernard Shaw

Have you overcome the uncertainties of growing up by paving a new direction for your future? The way we grow up stays with us forever and depending on whether our home life was a positive or negative experience instills much of the inner qualities that lead us through life. If we grew up in a negative or critical climate, the tension from the beginning of our lives played an important role in how we achieved or did not achieve our goals and dreams. Donald E. Sloat talked about the atmosphere of families in his book, *Growing Up Holy and Wholly*:

> Every family has a particular belief system with rules to guide domestic behavior and decisions. These basic beliefs set the tone for the families' activities and interests and determine the emotional atmospheres. These rules can be either healthy or dysfunctional… The dysfunctional types of rules provide destructive, emotionally unsafe atmospheres.[61]

Many times we do not know that our family was dysfunctional until we reach adulthood and the demons from our past interfere with our aspirations for our future. As much as we may not want to be like our parents, we often take on

---

[61] Donald E. Sloat, Ph.D., *Growing Up Holy & Wholly,* (Brentwood, Tennessee:, Wolgemuth & Hyatt, Publishers, Inc., 1990), 73-74.

their traits without thinking. Some of their traits and mannerisms are from learned behavior while others are genetically linked. Recognizing the negative traits that bothered us and then finding ways to overcome those same traits in our own lives is the only way to move forward. If we focus on the past and stew on the negativity that surrounded our youth, then we will become negative adults who accomplish nothing more than surviving from day to day. Our attitudes will allow no room for making every day count.

Former First Lady Barbara Bush spoke to a graduating class at Wellesley College and reminded them about the truly important things in life, which were families and relationships. She said:

> As important as your obligations as a doctor, lawyer, or business leader will be, you are a human being first, and those human connections—with spouses, with children, with friends—are the most important investments you will ever make. At the end of your life, you will never regret not having passed one more test, not winning one more verdict, or not closing one more deal. You will regret time not spent with a husband, a child, a friend, or a parent.[62]

Childhood is such a pivotal point in a person's life because it is where we learn about healthy and loving relationships or negative and dysfunctional ones. Those formative years tend to help us as we grow into contributing adults or hinder us from becoming anything but victims of the environment we were accustomed to. Living in the past and chewing the cud from a dysfunctional home can stall even the strongest person's ability to succeed, but there are ways to overcome the failures and sadness of the past as long as there is a breath of life. Today

---

[62] Stephen R. Covey, *7 Habits of Highly Effective Families*, (New York: Golden Books Publishing Co., Inc., 1997), 2.

could be the beginning of a new life by putting past mistakes, failures and unhappy moments behind. A person cannot get to the present or the future while remaining in the past. Focusing on the future is much more fulfilling to leading a life of purpose than focusing on all the mistakes or wrongs of the past.

If you are wrestling with a less than happy childhood, seek counsel from a professional and caring counselor. I have listed some organizations in Appendix A that can help you find the help you need to move forward.

Step Three: Adulthood

> *When one door closes another opens. But we often look so long and so regretfully upon the closed door that we fail to see the one that has opened for us.*
> –Alexander Graham Bell

Now that you have recognized your three greatest life achievements, think about how those feats were accomplished and what you can do to repeat those attitudes that helped you attain them. Accomplishing any success always involves some sort of effort and the only one who can make that happen is you. So if you have lost your zeal for life and cannot seem to move forward with your goals and desires, review those three achievements and remind yourself about what you did to make them happen. Look for ways to become inspired, either through prayer, inspirational reading or through life coaching. According to Success Counselor, Jim Rohn,

Inspiration…arouses feelings within us that rekindle hope, ambition and determination. It is a momentary whisper of encouragement and reassurance that causes us to become aware of our potential. We sense a spark of desire, and our minds flash from one possibility to another, each thought laden with the promise of future success and happiness. In this fleeting moment when inspiration stirs our soul we are either driven into action or we do nothing—being content to enjoy the warm feeling that is within us until, at last, the warmth moves on, taking with it the promise and the possibilities.[63]

The achievements you made were part inspiration, part calling and part timing, and there had to have been some sort of plan of action for you to accomplish them. Most likely those actions were not easy because they involved dedication, effort and determination—three traits that require energy and action. Goethe said, "Treat a man as he is and he will remain as he is. Treat a man as he can and should be, and he will become as he can and should be." The potential to break free from the chains that bind starts with a change of heart (Jesus Christ can offer that), a change in attitude (feelings dictate that), and a choice to change (freedom of will).

Lay out a strategy today for how you will accomplish your next opportunity. We often hear the saying, "Don't put off until tomorrow what you can accomplish today," but that saying leaves out the strategy for starting today. A person's biggest block in the road to achieving their goals and dreams is by saying, "**Someday**...I will go...or do...." You fill in the blanks. That one word tells yourself that you do not believe that you can really accomplish your dream. *Someday* is a procrastinator's biggest enemy because it lets a person off the hook from looking at the significance of today and focusing on how to make today that someday.

Today is the day to set a course and start climbing out of the trench that has left you feeling overwhelmed with life. Fill in the blanks of someday and put your plan of action in place. You have one day to start and today is that day.

---

[63] Jim Rohn, *The Five Major Pieces to the Life Puzzle,* (Southlake, TX: Dickinson Press, 1991*),* 45.

Step Four: Marriage

At the heart of mankind's existence is the desire to be intimate and to be loved by another. Marriage is designed to meet that need for intimacy and love.
                                             –Gary D. Chapman

Why are you married to your mate? This person was your choice for a lifelong partner, but now that she has put on 40 pounds and his hairline has more than receded and the kids are in your face constantly, romance and passion have been replaced by disgust and exhaustion. Forever seems like F-O-R-E-V-E-R; not a starry-eyed fantasy. Now that the wedding and honeymoon are memories locked away, the permanence of your decision has settled over your home, and it may feel like all the air that you breathed together as young lovers has been sucked away by a commercial-sized vacuum cleaner. Marriage is a long road with bumps, twists and turns, and if you are not prepared for it mentally and emotionally it can leave you defeated and deflated. Marriage and family experts John and Susan Yates explained marriage like this:

> Learning to be a good husband or wife…is like learning to swim long distances in deep water. If you are going to have a mature, loving, and truly good marriage and family life, you need to learn to "tread water" and "dog paddle" first.[64]

Like we discussed in Chapter 6, far more time is spent on the planning of the wedding than on the planning of the marriage. We didn't think about treading water and dog paddling before jumping into marriage because "we were in love." Most marriages produce children and becoming parents

---

[64] John and Susan Yates, *Building A Home Full of Grace,* (Grand Rapids, MI: Baker Books, 2003), 36.

puts undue stress on even the healthiest marriages. Dr. Alfred A. Nesser, a distinguished American physician, said:

> It is good to recall that marriage is permanent while parenthood is passing. Since marriage begins and ends with two, the primary concern is to keep that relationship in the best possible repair. Then, the parent-child relationship will take care of itself... Children are not meant to be the center of the family. That center is the relationship of husband and wife.[65]

Many times a marriage starts falling apart when the couple turns their focus away from each other and center all their attention on the children. And, as any parent knows, this is easy to do because if you give your child an inch, she will take a mile! Children come with demands, but husbands and wives need to learn to set aside marriage building time so the children will have a stable and unbroken home.

My husband and I were going through one of those down curves in our marriage when our house was filled with two toddlers and a baby who were constantly in need. Dan was building a business and trying to provide for us financially, and I was busy maintaining the daily ear infections, laundry, house, meals, and the overall safety and stability of our home. Our marriage was strained during those years, so in an effort to replace the love and happiness of days gone by, I found one of my favorite pictures of us on our honeymoon, framed it and put it in front of the kitchen sink. That was a reminder every day of the happiness that we had then and it reminded me of why I married Dan. This one picture points a course toward maintaining our commitment to the vows we exchanged and a means for keeping joy during the hard times. It still sits on our kitchen counter.

---

[65] Ibid., 39.

When you think about your marriage, are you looking at your spouse with eyes full of blame? Or, are you looking inward to what you have done to cause the downfall? How can any couple find romance again if they are constantly bickering or blaming each other for everything that is wrong? A marriage cannot be successful or lovingly survive without both partners putting forth the effort to make it work. Instead of blaming your spouse for your unhappiness, spend some time in front of the mirror and look at what you have done to contribute. It's not up to your partner to change, it's up to you to change and then maybe your spouse will notice the change in you and reciprocate. Don't expect change to happen overnight. It has probably taken years for your marriage to disintegrate and it will take a long time to build it back up.

Today is the day to change your attitude about your marriage and start working toward a more joyful union. By changing your attitude one day at a time and finding ways to rekindle your love and commitment, maybe you will break through those walls that have blocked out passion, harmony and contentment and find the love and peace you desire.

Step Five: Parenting

> *Things which matter most must never be at the mercy of things which matter least.*
>
> –Goethe

Remember Step One and the things you didn't like about your parents? Are you doing those same things as a parent? Parenting has to be the toughest job on the face of this earth. Children do not come out of the womb with a list of instructions for caring for their individual personalities and their human nature that was warped by the entrance of sin on the scene way back in the Garden of Eden. (We know all about Adam and Eve and that slimy serpent!) But children sure come into the world with a personality all their own. The challenges of parenting start with us; not with the children. Our attitude often determines their behaviors and their reactions. Jim Rohn described attitude in his book, *The Five Major Pieces to the Life Puzzle*:

> While philosophy deals essentially with the logical side of life—information and thinking habits—attitude focuses primarily on the emotional issues that affect our existence. What we know determines our philosophy. How we feel about what we know determines our attitude.[66]

Our reactions to parenting and attitude toward our children begin and end with us. It's not the ill behavior of our child, but our inability to change our attitude that robs us of the joy of parenting. The most important factor to parenting is obviously that of showing unconditional love; however, this does not mean using careful discipline. Without discipline, children will grow up without any regard for limitations. Dr. Henry Cloud and Dr. John Townsend wrote a book, *Boundaries with Kids*, where they establish the necessity of boundaries in parenting. They said,

> Parents are the source of all good things for a child. They are the bridge to the outside world of resources that sustain life. And in giving and receiving resources, boundaries play a very important role. Children need to learn how to receive and use responsibly what is given them and gradually take over the role of meeting their own needs. In the beginning, parents are the source; they progressively give the child the independence to obtain what they need on their own.[67]

---

[66]Jim Rohn, *The Five Major Pieces to the Life Puzzle* (Southlake, TX: Dickinson Press, 1991), 45.

[67] Dr. Henry Cloud and Dr. John Townsend, *Boundaries with Kids* (Grand Rapids, MI: Zondervan, 1998), 21.

Start today by listening to what your child is telling you and by setting realistic boundaries for the child and for you as the parent. Look deeply at that person and think of the gift of that beautiful life.

We long for our children to succeed and we encourage them to follow their dreams, but do they have a positive example to follow? Their best effort will happen when they see their parents' actions. Today is the day to start being a better parent. Take those steps toward developing a more nurturing parent/child relationship.

Chapter 17
The *One Day Method* for Life
Plan of Action

*The thing always happens that you really believe in;
and the belief in a thing makes it happen.*
–Frank Lloyd Wright

THE *ONE DAY METHOD* IS a tool designed to help you face your fears and your dreams, but as with any tool, if it is not used, it won't help. So to get started with your action plan, place a calendar in a conspicuous spot where you will have access to it every day. Then 30, 60 and 90 days into the future mark each of those dates with the words "One Day Checkpoint." For every day that you complete your daily goal, mark your calendar. When you get to each checkpoint, reread this section of the book and review the goals that you set for yourself. Evaluate how far you are in finding the real you and moving forward in your life. This is preparation for the rest of your life, and if you have been consistent in finding out what makes you tick, then you will be ready for a day when your life changes and you will have no regrets.

The Plan of Action is easy enough to follow because there is one item to help you through the step and then a prayer for the process. This model is a way to develop perseverance, determination and discipline so that you can follow through on a daily basis. Whatever you do, don't put the *One Day Method* on a shelf and forget about it, work through it so that you can find the significant life you have always craved.

Action Step One: Religious Beliefs

For the next 30 days:

Read two chapters of the New Testament each day—starting with Matthew. This will only take ten minutes of your day, but the impact of doing that will linger far beyond ten minutes and thirty days. If you cannot carve ten minutes out of your schedule, then buy the Bible on tape and listen to it on your daily commute.

Pray for guidance from God. Ask Him to give you faith and belief for the next 30 days and see if there is a change in your attitude and your beliefs. If you cannot take time to pray, make time by praying while taking your daily shower or for a few minutes before you get out of bed.

These two steps will take less than 15 minutes a day and they will help you begin to establish discipline by sticking to something consistently for 30 days. At the end of 30 days, review your spiritual goals and see if you are any closer to finding what you believe and believing what you found. Continue this discipline for another 30 days, and if you forget a day or two or three, don't beat yourself up, pick up and continue.

Action Step Two: Overcoming Childhood Barriers

For the next 30 days:

Each day write in your calendar or journal about one dream or idea that you had as a child. Focusing on the positive will help you get back to those dreams and encouraging feelings you had as a child and cultivate what is real and what was a fantasy.

Pray each day for freedom from the past and for a heart of forgiveness toward those who wronged you.

Often dreams we had as a child may have been our first clue

into who we are and who we wanted to become. After 30 days review the items in your journal and see if there is a pattern that you can follow, or find the one thing that sticks out more than any other. This could be the first step to fulfilling your dreams.

Action Step Three: Changing My Life as an Adult

For the next 30 days:
Write down two things you most desire to accomplish. Post those two things on your mirror where you can look at them each morning and evening when you are brushing your teeth. Say them out loud to yourself.

Pray for God's direction and will in accomplishing those things. Ask Him to give you a direction in how to attain your desires.

At the end of 30 days, how far have you come in investigating the means to achieve what you would like to achieve. If you haven't gotten anywhere, give yourself another 30 days, but remember that one day needs to be the beginning.

Action Step Four: Improving/Reviving Marriage Relationship

For the next 30 days:
Find and frame a picture of you and your spouse during the first month of marriage. Put the picture in a place where you will see it often throughout your day. (Picture frames, calendars and other *One Day* tools can be purchased from visiting my website: www.onedayliving.com.)

Pray for your spouse every time you look at that picture. Pray for your attitude and for restoration of love and commitment.

At the end of 30 days, share with your spouse about what you have done and ask him/her to join you in your endeavor to make your marriage better.

Action Step Five: Positive Parenting

For the next 30 days:
Write down one positive trait of each child.

Once a week for the next month after your children are in bed, go to each child's room and pray for that particular child and for your attitude for him. Pray for his personal needs. If your child is grown, take a picture and pray in the child's old room or wherever you are when he comes to mind.

At the end of 30 days review how you are responding as a parent and how your child is responding. Whether or not there is a change, continue the pattern for 30 more days and 30 more.

All of the things in this 5-step plan will take less than 20 minutes of your day. Is your life worth taking such a small amount of time to implement a discipline that will help you achieve your goals? Sure, it's much easier to not take the 20 minutes, but when the one day that changes your life happens, will you have those same regrets that I had when I saw my life flashing before my eyes?

Work your way through the *One Day Method* and make today the most significant day in your life so that you are ready to face tomorrow.

Chapter 18
The Fear of Change via Choice

One half of knowing what you want is knowing what you must give up before you get it.

–Sidney Howard

EVERY INDIVIDUAL THAT WE HAVE written about in this book made choices, and those choices determined their destiny. All of the decisions involved some form of change and, by learning from past experiences and lessons in history, we see that change is often painful. Overcoming the pain of past failures and mistakes is the biggest key to overcoming our lack of achievement. John Hancock had to change his whole thought pattern before he came to the table with his pen in hand on July 4, 1776. He wanted power and wealth for himself and did not necessarily want to be bogged down with political pressures from England or the colonials. General George Meade had not planned to encounter the Confederates at Gettysburg just days after he became a general, but his leadership and courage led the Union to defend against the advancing Confederates. President Franklin Roosevelt did not want to send American soldiers into World War II, but he was forced to change directions when America was attacked on December 7, 1941. President George W. Bush was faced with a grieving and scared nation after September 11, 2001, when the events forced him to change his focus by implementing a Division of Homeland Security which launched an all-out assault on terrorism.

In a book about the importance of every day, change is achievable when you realize that today counts and tomorrow is not guaranteed.

Now, the hard part will be to implement the changes from the *One Day Method*. Change is not always sudden, and it will take more time before results are witnessed; however, without a beginning there is no way to be successful in changing the direction. The Continental Congress signed *The Declaration of Independence* on July 4, 1776, but only after years of planning and fighting for it. The United States was not magically changed on that date either, but by the choice to act, the sovereignty was eventually gained. It is the same idea when a person wants to change course in the middle of his life. Often baby steps are required for success, but it is that ONE DAY that a decision was made to change that marks the course and sets the individual on the right path.

Most of the time, we do not achieve our dreams and goals because of our own fear of failure. Aren't we glad that fear of failure did not stop George Washington at The Battle of Trenton? Aren't we glad that fear of failure did not keep Abraham Lincoln from fighting to keep the Union? Aren't we glad that fear of failure did not keep Franklin Roosevelt from joining the battle to defeat the evil empires of Japan and Germany? Aren't we glad that fear of failure didn't keep George Bush from counterattacking the enemies in a strong effort to keep our shores safe? Aren't we glad that God did not turn His back on us because of our own fears and failures? Instead Christ went to the cross. All of these men laid more than their personal fears on the line; they had to carry a world through times of crises that made them unpopular and hated by some and honored and revered by others. But through the choices they made, they stood strong to protect the interests of the world.

Change and fear walk hand-in-hand with one another. The minute change comes along; fear jumps out and wiggles itself in the way of accomplishing anything. Fear of tomorrow, fear of failure or fear of success is not what we should be thinking about. The focus is to be prepared for tomorrow so that if a curve ball is thrown your way, you've already accomplished what is important and defined your purpose. Wouldn't you rather be prepared for the unexpected than fearful of it? I wish that I had started writing 15 years ago when I was in my early twenties and I had a lot more time on my hands (I just didn't know that!), but fear of failure and the never ending pile of bills kept me from pursuing my writing career. I would have preferred to have been writing long before I got cancer, not because of it.

In my opinion, fear and unbelief are the main reasons that Jesus was and still is rejected. Even when people witnessed his miracles and an empty tomb, their fear kept them from their faith. Faith is always a part of change. If God had told all there was to know about His plan for Jesus, for us and for the world, faith would not be needed and life would not require any effort on our part.

We have two choices: to live in fear and never live up to our full potential, or to break free from those fears and live out our goals. What is your choice?

Chapter 19
The Nation, The Person, The Decision, The Method

The only limit to our realization of tomorrow will be our doubts
of today. Let us move forward with strong and active faith.
　　　　　　　　　　　　　　　　　　－Franklin Delano Roosevelt

THROUGHOUT THIS BOOK WE HAVE noted significant
dates in the lives of individuals and dates that have affected our
nation and our world. We all have dates that stand out more
than others, and each one of those days represent an element of
our life and signifies the importance of that time. But, isn't
every day just as important?

The Nation

July 4, 1776, would not have happened if brave and
headstrong men backed by ordinary citizens had not made the
conscious choice to stand up for their beliefs by focusing on
principle and making a decision. The result of that decision
made by men of character changed the course of our world, as
we know it.

July 3, 1863, General Robert E. Lee made a decision that
cost him a turning point battle in the sad and long Civil War.
The choice to have Pickett take 15,000 men out in the open and
charge up Cemetery Ridge, may have changed the course of a
war that could have divided our country into two separate
nations and left an ethnic group enslaved instead of liberated.

December 7, 1941, forced the United States to stand for liberty across the world. America's choice was decided for her when she was thrust into battle by the deafening cries of the sailors that died with their ships in the bloody waters of Pearl Harbor.

September 11, 2001, awoke Americans to the realities of evil when our innocence was once again stolen from our shores as we watched the crumbling towers fall and people's lives from New York to Washington, D.C., shattered into millions of pieces of ruins.

We have noted just four days that wrote American history. There were choices made by many people before those dates ever occurred and that is what made the people and the dates standout and that determined the future of our nation.

The Person

In your life there are birthdays, anniversaries and holidays that mark the extraordinary circumstance surrounding each day. It's a part of life, as we know it to celebrate the dates that we hold close. Without those momentous celebrations, life would feel empty and hopeless. The dreams of tomorrow and the plans that we make are what keep the cycle of life moving. Making arrangements for weekend barbeques, birthday parties and wedding festivities keep the spirit of life alive and make living enjoyable. Momentous occasions mold and shape us into the individuals that embody the earth. There is a reason for all things and there is a meaning to our lives, even if we cannot always figure it out.

Your birthday was significant because without your mother and father making the conscious (or unconscious) decision to have a child, you were formed, whether planned or unplanned—you arrived to become a part of the human race.

When you graduated, you embarked on adulthood and started heading for the future. Perhaps years later you are not where you dreamed at 20 years old you would be, but you made twists and turns along the way that brought you to where you are and your education was a critical factor in that choice.

Your wedding day was a day that bound you to another person for better or worse and from that point forward all decisions made affected not just one person but two. It was the day that brought about a celebration and a new family.

The day you or a loved one received a life-threatening diagnosis changed all the priorities and focus of your life around. The small things that seem big are unimportant and the big thing is living life to its fullest. Your perception of what is important has been forever altered and fear has a new meaning.

The day your loved one died is a date of sadness and mourning; reflection and memory recollection. Every year that day is remembered as you ponder the loss and grieve once more for that special person; knowing that someday you will die too and leave someone grieving for you. The cycle of life is very real when we lose a loved one to death.

The Decision

We have researched the life of Jesus Christ according to Biblical history and questioned why His life was important then and why He is still celebrated today. His life has caused more debate than any other. Was he God or was he just a moral teacher and prophet? Would a moral teacher or prophet claim to be God if he was not? History could not be molded and determined by a mere prophet or moral teacher who lied about being God. The claim must be genuine. The life of Christ has been documented and studied from the time He walked the earth and will continue to be the most sought out conclusion for the rise of Christianity. This book's purpose is not to compare religious leaders who have risen up during different eras with Jesus, but if a comparison were to be made—no other religious leader has stood the test of time through thousands of years, changed the calendar, or changed the lives of millions who have followed Him by faith.

C.S. Lewis stated in his book, *Mere Christianity,*

> I am trying here to prevent anyone saying the really foolish thing that people often say about Him: "I'm ready to accept Jesus as a great moral teacher, but I don't accept His claim to be God." That is the one thing we must not say. A man who was merely a man and said the sort of things Jesus said would not be a great moral teacher. He would either be a lunatic—on a level with the man who says he is a poached egg—or else he would be the Devil of Hell. You must make your choice. Either this man was, and is, the Son of God: or else a madman or something worse. You can shut Him up for a fool, you can spit at Him and kill Him as a demon; or you can fall at His feet and call Him Lord and God. But let us not come with any patronizing nonsense about His being a great human teacher. He has not left that open to us. He did not intend to.[68]

Now the most significant date in your life is based on your choice to accept His Word and have faith and trust that what He said is true. Today could be the day that changes not only your life now, but also your destiny tomorrow. It's not how you live, but how you choose to live and whom you choose to live for.

The Method

There are many tools available at the library, local bookstore, and churches that can help us become "all that" and more, but you are the only person that can improve your situation. You don't have to do it alone—that is why faith is

[68] C.S. Lewis, *Mere Christianity* (New York: Macmillan Publishing Company, 1960), 56.

important to make you a person of significance and change the direction of your life. The more we try to improve ourselves on our own, the more we will fail, but the more we include the most important factor—Jesus Christ—we will be able to see ourselves for who God wanted us to become. Although you will see results if you work with the *One Day Method* on your own, the biggest result will be including this personal relationship. If you have already dedicated your life to Christ, then the *One Day Method* will have a new meaning and may lead you in a different direction because everything you can achieve should be to please God and not for your own selfish motives. Achieving a better life is not a material process but a spiritual one. Think how that direction can change your life!

Conclusion

What God expects us to attempt,
He also enables us to achieve.
                              –Stephen Olford

EACH DAY BRINGS NEW CIRCUMSTANCES and unexpected happenings. When we open our eyes in the morning we are faced with a day full of choices and ultimately, we are the one who decides. Significant dates all stem from the choices that each one of us makes.

Some time ago my husband and I were discussing life, and he began explaining his metaphor for life as a ship setting sail. He described the optimism of sailing on calm clear waters with sunny skies and a charted course, but then further out to sea the storms start rolling in and the thunderous waves batter and toss the ship. When the storm clears there is a broken mast and battered ship and then calm seas return and doldrums set in.

Our conversation continued and he asked me, "What is your metaphor for life?"

After careful thought, I responded, "Life is a beautifully wrapped gift."

Each day the package is laid before us in all of its colorful wrappings and the moment our minds can form a conscious image of the day is the moment we have started taking the wrappings off the package to peek inside. The box reads 'Fragile: Handle with Care' and we go about each day making decisions, breathing, laughing, crying, smiling, sighing, but the package holds a new day and what we do with that package is largely up to us.

Think about your reaction when you receive a gift. Are you the type of person that opens your presents carefully saving the paper while you drive everyone else crazy with anticipation? Or do you rip and tear at the paper in an exhilarating rush to see what's inside? The gift of life can be lived so many ways, but each person determines what he or she sees in the daily package. Is there negativity from day to day hiding within the tissue paper? Maybe within the folds of your life there is overwhelming bitterness and a boatload of excuses that blame everyone else but you for your view of life and the mistakes you've made that have left you feeling empty.

Within every day's gift are decisions involving your reaction. In the folds of tissue paper there are the elements of peace, contentment, joy, optimism and love. A pessimistic view isn't a part of the gift God gives us; it's a part of our human nature. The worry, complaining, fear, and bitterness are not in the reward of each morning—they are embedded in our heads from living in a fallen world. God provided us with a way to get rid of those old tendencies by offering Jesus Christ as our gift for every day. Through a life lived for Christ, we can throw away the past and replace it with the new gift. If we receive a new watch as a gift, will we leave it in the box and continue to wear an old watch that does not keep the correct time? It's the same with the gift of life.

I could not always say I viewed life as a gift. I was a person who blamed others for my lack of accomplishing goals that I had set out to achieve. Those excuses that I had concocted in my head were the storms on the sea and the doldrums of self-pity. I wrote a poem describing that view:

The Vision In My Head

I had a vision in my head of who I wanted to be
   What I wanted to do in life and how I would succeed
The vision is from another day long before this one
   It's when my future brought forth promises
   And my goals and dreams were on the run.

I have a vision in my head—now that I am an adult
   Of days gone by and wasted by focusing on my faults.
The vision makes me feel like a failure many times
   It often overtakes my eagerness and drive
   And comes at me from behind.

This vision in my head needs to be defeated once and for all
   Before it takes over my spirit and I permanently fall
The vision in my head must be replaced by another
   One that will provide clarity for the present
   And a future full of summers.

The vision in my heart needed to be refined
   But it was buried by negative feelings for a very long time.
The vision in my heart came when I humbly bowed
   And let go of the past's mistakes
   By taking a hold of what I have now.

While undergoing chemotherapy treatments, I began viewing life as a gift because my mortality had surfaced. Fortunately my prognosis was positive with expectancy for survival—unlike many other diseases and accidents that take life in an instant. During those months, I had to remain focused and strong by succumbing to actually being physically weak and yielding control of my body to God. As a cancer survivor, it is still up to me to view each day as another beautiful present given by God to marvel and celebrate. Going through that experience in 2002 only strengthened my determination to cherish every moment and push negative thoughts and complaints from my mind.

Since he was a little boy, our son, Tyler, has been a thinker. One day as he was deep in thought, I asked him what he was thinking about, and his five-year-old response was, "I'm thinking about what I'm thinking about."

I've always remembered that, and that was exactly what I had to do as I faced the uncertainty of cancer. I had to think about what I was thinking about so that I could get through the ordeal. It was at the frightening point of having cancer that I decided that I would not let fear of cancer rob me of the joy of living.

Are you going to let fear rob you of the joy of fulfilling your dreams and making a better life for you, your children and your family? Maybe it's time to start thinking about what you are thinking about.

Rick Warren frankly said in his book, *The Purpose Driven Life*, "The fear of what we might discover if we honestly faced our character defects keeps us living in the prison of denial."[69]

That was me. I was afraid to try to change and afraid of the effects of change, so I lived in a state of denial of what my

---

[69] Rick Warren, *The Purpose Driven Life*, (Grand Rapids: Zondervan, 2002), 220.

dreams were and of what I hoped to accomplish in life. In essence I kept myself from thinking because I was afraid to face it. Fear and change are always battling. When we long to change and grow, fear is often the strongest factor in holding us back from making those changes. However, we have the upper hand to control our fear and make the choices that will further change.

Warren went further and said, "There is no growth without change; there is no change without fear or loss; and there is no loss without pain."[70]

Growth requires change and pain, and sadness and pain are parts of life. No one gets through life without facing sorrow and hurt. Sometimes through the pain and fear we cannot see the positive side of life and through our grief and despair we succumb to worry, bitterness, and anger. Those times are the stormy seas that the ship must encounter, but the calm sea is right around the corner and within our grasp—it is the gift of life. Each morning, when you first open your eyes, look at the beautifully wrapped gift sitting beside your bed and decide how you will view what's inside that day.

So what difference did today make in my life? This book is the result of January 8, 2002. If I had not faced and battled cancer, I would still be dreaming about the day I would become a writer. That day made me realize I may not have tomorrow to become a writer, but only today. Unfortunately, I needed something earth shattering to force me to act. Fortunately I survived, and because of that I wanted to share with others that waiting for someday is not the way to go. Do not wait for that life-changing event before you improve your life. You only have today to make decisions that can affect your tomorrows. Today is significant. The cycle of life continues, and this very

---

[70] Ibid., 220.

day as you open the gift and pick through the tissue papers of your package, what will you find there?

Write it on your heart that every day is the best day in the year.
                                                    –Ralph Waldo Emerson

Appendix A

Throughout the *One Day Method* portion of the book, you may have encountered the need for help dealing with the past. These organizations offer encouragement to the discouraged and have highly trained and credentialed counselors to help. They work nationally and internationally.

Focus on the Family
www.family.org
1-800-232-6459

FamilyLife
www.familylife.com
1-800-358-6329

Smalley Relationship Center
www.smalley.gospelcom.net
1-800-848-6329